How to Research
the Presidency

How to Research the Presidency

Fenton S. Martin
Robert U. Goehlert
Indiana University

Congressional Quarterly Inc.
Washington, D.C.

Copyright © 1996 Congressional Quarterly Inc.

Printed in the United States of America

Library of Congress Cataloging-in-Publication Data

Martin, Fenton S.
    How to research the presidency / Fenton S. Martin, Robert U. Goehlert.
       p.   cm.
    Includes bibliographical references and indexes.
    ISBN 1-56802-029-5 — ISBN 1-56802-028-7 (pbk.)
    1. Presidents—United States—Bibliography.   2. Presidents—United
States—Research.   I. Goehlert, Robert.   II. Title.
  Z1249.P7M365   1996
  [JK516]
  016.973—dc20   96-7488
                                          CIP

Contents

Preface   ix

Introduction   1

    Types of Legal Sources   1
    Designing a Research Strategy   2

Secondary Sources and Finding Tools   5

    Almanacs   5
    Factbooks   6
    Biographical Directories   7
    Dictionaries   8
    Handbooks   8
    Encyclopedias   9
    Bibliographies   9
    Indexes   10
    Compact Disk Products   13
    Databases   15
    Journals   16
    Newsmagazines   18
    Newspapers and Indexes   19
    News Services   19
    Statistical Sources   20

Primary Sources and Finding Tools   21

    Researching the Presidency   21
      Research Guides to Government Publications   22
      Guides to the Presidency   23
      Presidential Publications   23
        Legislative and Administrative Papers   24
        Foreign Affairs   24
        Messages   25

Textual Sources	25
Indexes to Texts	28
Information Sources on the Presidency	34
Speeches and Press Conferences	34
Vetoes	36
Presidential Advisory Commissions	36
Executive Office	38
Platforms	40
Campaigns	41
Election Returns	42
Television Coverage	46
Oral Histories	47
Interest Groups	47
Public Opinion Polls	48
Audiovisual Materials	49
Internet Sources	50
Archives	52
Data Archives	55
Administrative Law	55
Finding Tools	57
Statutory Law	58
Finding Tools	58
Legislative Histories	60
Case Law	61
Digests of Supreme Court Decisions	63
Briefs and Records of the Supreme Court	63

Selected Bibliography on the Presidency and Presidents

	65
Perspectives on the Presidency	65
The Presidency and the Constitution	68
Presidential Powers	69
Presidential Leadership	71
Presidential Character	72
The President and the Executive Branch	73
The Cabinet	73
The White House Staff	73
The White House Advisors	74
The Vice Presidency	74
Management of the Bureaucracy	75

Policymaking   75
  The President and Foreign Policy   76
  War-Making Powers   78
  Executive Agreements   78
  National Security Policy   79
  The President and Domestic Policy   79

The President and Congress   80
The President and the Judiciary   83
Presidential Media Coverage   83
Public Opinion of Presidents   84
The Selection of Presidents   85
  Primaries   87
  Conventions   87
  Campaign Debates   88
  Campaign Finances   88
  The Media and Presidential Selection   88
  Voting in Presidential Elections   89
  The Electoral College   90
  Presidential Election Studies   91

Presidential Transitions   92
Presidential Succession   92
The Presidents   93
  George Washington   93
  John Adams   93
  Thomas Jefferson   94
  James Madison   95
  James Monroe   95
  John Quincy Adams   96
  Andrew Jackson   96
  Martin Van Buren   97
  William Henry Harrison   97
  John Tyler   97
  James K. Polk   98
  Zachary Taylor   98
  Millard Fillmore   98
  Franklin Pierce   98
  James Buchanan   99
  Abraham Lincoln   99
  Andrew Johnson   100
  Ulysses S. Grant   100
  Rutherford B. Hayes   101
  James A. Garfield   101
  Chester A. Arthur   101
  Grover Cleveland   102
  Benjamin Harrison   102

William McKinley   102
Theodore Roosevelt   102
William Howard Taft   103
Woodrow Wilson   103
Warren G. Harding   104
Calvin Coolidge   105
Herbert Hoover   105
Franklin D. Roosevelt   106
Harry S. Truman   107
Dwight D. Eisenhower   108
John F. Kennedy   108
Lyndon B. Johnson   109
Richard M. Nixon   110
Gerald R. Ford   110
Jimmy Carter   111
Ronald Reagan   111
George Bush   112
Bill Clinton   112

Appendix   113
U.S. Presidents and Vice Presidents   114
Backgrounds of U.S. Presidents   116
Glossary   120

Index   127
Author Index   127
Title Index   129

Preface

How to Research the Presidency offers an introduction to basic research resources on the presidency. We present a variety of resources available to the researcher to aid in presidential study. These include specific guides to locating or interpreting presidential documents as well as general guide books to government and legal resources. Materials providing background information on the presidency and current events have been added as well. The resources we have included were selectively chosen and the accompanying annotations have been kept as simple as possible.

We begin the book by presenting secondary sources and the finding tools used to locate them. These sources include almanacs, dictionaries, encyclopedias, and biographical sources that provide background or historical information about the presidency. In addition, news publications, including newspapers, newsmagazines, news services, and journals contain current information on the presidency. Pertinent indexes, abstracting services, online databases, and CD-ROM products are also described. Knowing which publications and services are available is key not only to pinpointing specific information but to simplifying the research process as well.

The second part of this book covers primary sources and the finding tools used to locate them. We describe a variety of guides that present an overview of the type and variety of presidential publications available to the legal researcher. This is followed by a discussion of specific sources useful in finding information on the presidency. Finally, we identify the finding tools necessary for locating administrative law, statutory law, and case law, all of which are integral to effective legal research.

In the third part of this book we offer a selected bibliography of major books about the presidency and the presidents. Topic areas include the history of the presidency and its development, powers, and relations with the legislative and judicial branches of government. We've also included a glossary, appendixes, an author index, and a title index.

Our intent is to assist both the general reader and the researcher interested in the presidency. We have listed those materials that are commercially available and that can be found in academic and public libraries.

We wish to thank the Political Science Department at Indiana University for its support of our research. Thanks to Steve Flinn (systems manager) for his technical assistance. Special thanks go to Richard Pacelle for answering questions about the presidency. Once again, we were fortunate to have Tracy Villano work as copy editor on one of our books. We highly value her expertise. Thanks go to the production editor, Talia Greenberg, who saw our work go from manuscript to book.

Introduction

The study of the presidency relies upon a distinct body of literature that can be used to develop a topic and formulate a research strategy. The approach you choose can both shape and focus your research. For example, a legal analysis might emphasize the statutory history, whereas an institutional approach might focus on organizational behavior. In either case the primary and secondary sources drawn upon will vary. It is important to consider what resources are available before setting out to conduct research, as not every library will have all the sources cited in this book.

Types of Legal Sources

The three types of legal sources are primary sources, secondary sources, and finding tools. These include books, articles, databases, newspapers, indexes, reference tools, and CD-ROMs. Some sources include both primary and secondary sources; some contain primary and secondary sources and finding tools as well.

Primary legal sources are publications by government bodies. Administrative regulations, rules, decisions, treaties, executive and legislative documents, and judicial opinions and reports are all primary legal sources. They range in time from the first federal laws and judicial opinions to the rulings and decisions of yesterday. Since primary legal sources remain in force until they are overruled or repealed, it is important that even the earliest primary legal sources remain accessible.

Secondary legal sources explain, interpret, and update primary sources. They can be interpretive, analytical, or critical in nature. Administrative reports, briefs and opinions, dictionaries, encyclopedias, and periodicals are examples of secondary legal sources. These sources can sometimes be used as finding tools to locate additional material.

Finding tools help the researcher locate or update primary and secondary sources. These include indexes to presidential publications and research guides. Because most primary legal sources are issued chronologically, some means of subject access into this large body of literature is necessary. The subject approach to legal sources allows the researcher to find existing presidential publications. Finding tools that provide subject access include encyclopedias; research guides; bibliographies; indexes to rules, statutes, and decisions; periodical indexes; and online database services such as LEXIS/NEXIS, WESTLAW, CQ's WASHINGTON ALERT, and LEGI-SLATE.

Designing a Research Strategy

The research strategy you develop will determine the kinds of materials you will seek. In this section, we present an outline on how to develop a topic and design a strategy for researching the presidency.

Your first challenge is to develop a topic that is sufficiently narrow, manageable, and original. Topics generally grow from some unanswered question warranting further analysis or explanation. If you already have an idea about something to investigate, you are well on your way. However, if you have not come across a questionable statement or one you think is too simple, then you will have to create a topic. The best method is to browse through current newspapers, books, bibliographies, or a periodical index to see what is being written about the presidency. You should look for an interesting action or event that you would like to analyze, evaluate, or explain. Then do some initial research to see what books and articles have been written about that particular subject. This type of preliminary research will help you develop your topic.

Developing questions regarding a particular action or event may involve combining one event with another or combining an event with a concept. As you develop your topic, keep in mind that you will need to define a proposition or hypothesis to prove or disprove. You should also think about describing the topic, such as when it took place, who was involved, why it was considered a problem, who was affected, and so on. The more you think about a topic and outline the details, the easier it will be to search thoroughly and systematically for relevant material.

Secondary sources can also be useful in directing your research. Encyclopedias, dictionaries, and journal articles can lead you to important primary sources by identifying, for example, key presidential advisors or White House staff.

Once you have a topic, but before you begin to search for additional materials, you should think through a basic research design. This will help you to organize your research strategy and clarify your topic. If the topic is too broad, you will need to scale back. If a proposition cannot be argued effectively, you will have to select another hypothesis. A research design should include a statement of the topic, a review of the literature, a definition of the hypothesis to be tested, a description of the operational design, and the methods of analysis and interpretation.

A checklist of the kinds of materials you are looking for and the specific finding tools necessary to gain access to those materials will help to focus your strategy. It should identify which significant facts and legal issues need to be researched. It is also important to think about which disciplines, such as law, history, or political science, you might explore for material, as well as the period you will cover (one year, a decade). Outlining a research strategy ahead of time will make your library search more efficient and productive. Begin your search by checking several basic finding tools.

1. Search the library's subject catalog.
2. Search periodical indexes and abstracting services, either in print, on CD-ROM, or on online format.
3. Search online information services, such as LEXIS/NEXIS, CQ's WASHINGTON ALERT, LEGI-SLATE, and WESTLAW.
4. Search the Internet for any pertinent information.
5. Search encyclopedias and dictionaries for background information and citations to primary sources.
6. Search newspaper indexes for information on the topic.
7. Search for bibliographies on the topic.
8. Search research guides to identify any compilations, handbooks, almanacs, and other finding tools particularly germane to the topic.
9. Check bibliographies and footnotes in books, articles, dissertations, and other materials you will use to begin your research. These can lead to important secondary sources.
10. Make a list of primary sources, including speeches, press conferences, executive orders, and so forth, identified through secondary sources. Write down the dates when actions occurred and who was involved.
11. Search the appropriate finding tools for identifying government documents.
12. Gather and analyze the documents.

A list of all possible terms, concepts, and names that you will check for as subject headings can be invaluable. It may include as many as a dozen or more possible subject headings. Because subject headings vary depending on which finding tool they are in, you will need to think of synonyms for a comprehensive search. As you continue your research, you will find which subject headings are most useful. A common mistake is to look under just one or two subject headings, find only a few citations, and assume that little has been written about the topic. While that may be the case, many times the materials are indexed under other subject headings. If you are using tools that allow key word searching, keep track of which terms you have used. If your finding tools have both subject and key word searching, try both approaches.

Keeping a record of your research makes it easier to revise your strategy or refer back to a source to get additional citations or information. While conducting your search be sure to take notes and make a record of where you have found specific citations. Such a record will save you time and facilitate your writing later on.

Secondary Sources and Finding Tools

In this section we offer a list of selected reference books and services that are useful in conducting research on the presidency. The entries are grouped by category, and most include a brief description.

Almanacs

Almanacs are useful as ready reference sources. Although a variety of formats are used, these almanacs contain similar information.

Congress and the Nation. 8 vols. Washington, DC: Congressional Quarterly, 1945–1993.
    This well-organized reference set provides quick access to descriptions of major legislation and issues in the Congress, White House, and Supreme Court. The work offers an excellent chronological history of major legislative programs and political developments during each Congress and executive administration, including biographical information, major votes, key judicial decisions, and election issues. An additional volume is published every four years.

Congressional Quarterly Almanac. Washington, DC: Congressional Quarterly, 1945—.
    This annual reference summarizes the work of the federal government for the previous year. Included are accounts of presidential programs and initiatives, major legislation enacted, analyses of Supreme Court decisions, election results of any federal elections held in the last year, an examination of lobbying activities, and other special reports.

Washington Almanac: A Guide to Federal Policy. New York: Holt, 1992—.
This annual volume offers analyses of current issues and touches
upon every major policy concern of government. The work
includes biographical profiles of more than 350 administration
officials, lobbyists, and policymakers.

Factbooks

Factbooks provide both biographical information and factual data.
They are excellent starting points for researching basic questions.

Kane, Joseph N. *Facts About the Presidents: A Compilation of Biographical and
Historical Data*. 6th ed. New York: H. W. Wilson, 1993.
This factbook contains short biographies of each president from
Washington to Clinton. Information about social and family background and a profile of the administration are contained in each
sketch. Administration data include the composition of the cabinet, Supreme Court appointments, the party leadership within
the House and Senate for each Congress, and significant dates
and events. There is also a short description of elections, including the names of all candidates contending for the office as well as
the electoral results. A section of comparative data focuses on a
wide range of information, such as cultural and vocational backgrounds, religious affiliations, and books authored by the presidents. The work also examines the presidency as an institution.

Wilson, Vincent. *The Book of the Presidents*. 9th ed. Brookeville, MD: American History Research, 1985.
This book is a compendium of facts and lore about the presidents
from Washington to Nixon. Separate chapters are devoted to
each president and include biographical data, significant public
achievements prior to election, and information on the administration. Additional facts on elections, conventions, inaugurations,
vice presidents, cabinets, and the Supreme Court are provided
as well. The work has several appendices: a chronological key to
the Congress, administrations, and constitutional amendments;
major acts and treaties; and a statistical summary. While a valuable
general source, it does not provide detailed historical coverage.

Three additional general factbooks are listed below:

Paletta, Lu Ann. *World Almanac of Presidential Facts*. Rev. ed. New York:
Pharos, 1993.

Whitney, David C. *The American Presidents*. New York: Prentice-Hall, 1990.

World Book of America's Presidents. 2 vols. Chicago: World Book Encyclopedia, 1994.

Biographical Directories

These tools direct a researcher to information about the president, White House staff, and other key executive branch officials.

Almanac of the Executive Branch. Washington, DC: Almanac Publishing, Inc., 1995—.
This almanac includes over five hundred profiles of cabinet- and subcabinet-level appointees. The profiles offer information on professional background, past political experience, and education and discuss the responsibilities of the position. The work also provides organizational charts for each agency as well as a brief history.

Federal Staff Directory. Mt. Vernon, VA: Staff Directories, Ltd., 1982—.
This directory lists federal workers in the executive branch, including those in all of the departments and in both independent and quasi-official agencies. Biographies of key federal executives and an index of individuals are provided. The *Federal Staff Directory* is published every March and September and is available from the publisher on disk, entitled *Federal Staff Directory on Disk*. The company publishes the *Federal Staff Directory* on CD-ROM. This product also includes the *Congressional Staff Directory* and the *Judicial Staff Directory*. The CD-ROM is entitled Staff Directories on CD-ROM PLUS. The *Federal Staff Directory* is available on-line through LEGI-SLATE.

O'Brien, Steven. *American Political Leaders: From Colonial Times to the Present*. Santa Barbara, CA: ABC-Clio, 1991.
This volume includes biographies of presidents, vice presidents, secretaries of state, Speakers, and chief justices as well as of members of Congress, ambassadors, and various other individuals.

Sobel, Robert. *Biographical Directory of the United States Executive Branch, 1774–1989*. 2d ed. Westport, CT: Greenwood Press, 1990.
This directory of executive branch officials includes birth dates and educational, social, political, and career information. Each biography contains a short bibliographic reference to important

primary and secondary resources. This work includes eight appendices: presidential administrations; heads of state and cabinet officials; other federal government service; state, county, and municipal government service; military service by branch; education; place of birth; and marital information. There are over 650 biographies of individuals who have served in the executive branch.

In addition to the above directories, the following works provide the same kind of material and are especially useful for finding information about federal staff throughout the executive branch.

The Capitol Source. Washington, DC: National Journal, 1986—.

The Federal Yellow Book: A Directory of the Federal Departments and Agencies. New York: Leadership Directories, 1977—.

Who's Who in the Federal Executive Branch. Washington, DC: Congressional Quarterly, 1993—.

Dictionaries

Dictionaries on the presidency can be used for finding answers to ready reference questions, such as dates, terms, concepts, definitions, and information about individuals.

Elliot, Jeffrey M., and Sheikh R. Ali. *The Presidential Congressional Political Dictionary.* Santa Barbara, CA: ABC-Clio, 1984.
This dictionary contains twelve subject chapters. Entries are arranged alphabetically within each chapter, and most offer numerous cross references. A detailed index that includes the dictionary entries as well as reference to specific information, such as individuals or organizations, is provided.

Handbooks

Handbooks contain essays on the history and development of the presidency as well as on approaches to researching it.

Edwards, George C., John H. Kessel, and Bert A. Rockman. *Researching the Presidency: Vital Questions, New Approaches.* Pittsburgh: University of Pittsburgh Press, 1993.

This excellent volume summarizes and evaluates the state of research on the presidency. It explores new ideas and theoretical
perspectives for studying the presidency with the hope of gener-
ating new approaches.

Graff, Henry F., ed. *The Presidents: A Reference History*. 2d ed. New York:
Scribner's, 1996.
This volume provides an overview and critical evaluation of each
president and administration. It is in essence a biography of each
presidential administration.

Encyclopedias

Encyclopedias are especially useful for finding basic information,
such as dates, names, and significant events. The following are two excellent encyclopedias on the presidency.

Levy, Leonard W., and Louis Fisher, eds. *Encyclopedia of the American Presidency*. New York: Simon and Schuster, 1994.
This four-volume set contains more than one thousand original
essays on the presidency. Fully cross-referenced and providing a
comprehensive index of terms, concepts, names, and court cases,
this is the definitive encyclopedia on the history, power, and politics of the presidency. It covers domestic and foreign policy, economic issues, votes, vetoes, and every presidential election.

The Presidency A to Z: A Ready Reference Encyclopedia. Washington, DC:
Congressional Quarterly, 1994.
This volume's approximately three hundred entries provide an
overview of the presidency, including its powers, history, and development. Entries encompass subjects such as appointment and
removal powers, assassinations, and national party conventions.
Biographies of all of the presidents and vice presidents appear as
well. The entries are alphabetically arranged and cross refer-
enced. The volume includes extensive indexes and appendices.

Bibliographies

The bibliographies noted here cover a variety of material, including books, journal literature, dissertations, and selected government
documents.

The American Presidency: A Historical Bibliography. Santa Barbara, CA: ABC-Clio, 1984.
  This bibliography consists of more than three thousand abstracts from journals in the social sciences and humanities published between 1973 and 1982. It covers the lives of presidents, presidential elections, and the growth of the executive branch and features a multiterm subject index.

Martin, Fenton S., and Robert U. Goehlert. *The American Presidency: A Bibliography.* Washington, DC: Congressional Quarterly, 1987.
  This bibliography on the presidency provides citations to books, dissertations, journal articles, research reports, and selected documents. It includes citations of materials published up to 1987. This work is a companion volume to Martin and Goehlert's *American Presidents: A Bibliography.* By using both resources, a researcher can easily identify all of the books, articles, and dissertations written about the presidency.

Martin, Fenton S., and Robert U. Goehlert. *American Presidents: A Bibliography.* Washington, DC: Congressional Quarterly, 1987.
  This bibliography includes citations to books, journal articles, research reports, and dissertations written about each president. It contains materials published up to 1987. This work is a companion volume to Martin and Goehlert's *The American Presidency: A Bibliography.* By using both resources, a researcher can easily identify all of the books, articles, and dissertations written about the presidency.

Indexes

Indexes and abstracting services are crucial for finding journal articles on the presidency. Many indexes are now available on CD-ROM, which can save time and effort. The following printed indexes are the most useful for finding journal articles pertaining to the presidency.

ABC POL SCI: A Bibliography of Contents: Political Science and Government. Santa Barbara, CA: ABC-Clio, 1969—.
  Tables of contents from journals, both U.S. and foreign, are published six times a year in this index. Because it is published in advance of the journals' publication dates, this index is especially useful for finding very recent articles on the presidency. It is available on CD-ROM and as an online database.

America: History and Life. Santa Barbara, CA: ABC-Clio, 1964—.
Articles, book and film reviews, and dissertations are covered in this serial bibliography. A streamlined format adopted in 1989 offers quarterly indexes containing abstracts and citations. There is also a cumulative annual index. This abstracting service provides excellent coverage of materials in the field of history as well as political science and the social sciences in general. You should always include this index for historical research on the presidency. It is available on CD-ROM and as an online database.

Current Law Index. Menlo Park, CA: Information Access Corp., 1980—.
This monthly paper index covers legal periodicals and newspapers. Its microfilm counterpart, *Legal Resources Index*, cumulates the information found in the paper copy. *Legal Resources Index* is available on CD-ROM, where it is called LegalTrac. This index should be consulted for any literature search on the presidency.

Humanities Index. New York: H. W. Wilson, 1974—.
This is a quarterly index to English-language journals in the humanities. The articles are indexed by author and subject. Covering the major history journals, this index is best used in searches for citations related to the history of the presidency. It is available on CD-ROM and as an online database.

Index to Legal Periodicals. New York: H. W. Wilson, 1908—.
This monthly resource indexes articles appearing in the legal periodicals of the United States, Canada, Great Britain, Northern Ireland, Australia, and New Zealand. Indexes are provided for authors, subjects, book reviews, and cases. This resource should be used in almost every literature search on the presidency. Since it is one of the oldest legal indexes, it can be used for historical research as well. *Index to Legal Periodicals* is available on CD-ROM and as an online database.

International Political Science Abstracts. Paris: International Political Science Association, 1951—.
This bimonthly work abstracts articles published in English-language and foreign-language political science journals. The abstracts for the English-language journals appear in English and the foreign-language articles are abstracted in French. This abstracting service is the best source for finding foreign-language articles about the presidency. Even if you are not interested in foreign-language material, you should check to see if this service

has citations on the presidency that have not appeared in other indexes. *International Political Science Abstracts* is available on CD-ROM.

Public Affairs Information Service Bulletin (PAIS). New York: PAIS, 1915—.
This weekly subject guide to American politics in general indexes government publications, books, and periodical literature. It also indexes the *National Journal,* the *Congressional Quarterly Weekly Report,* the *Congressional Digest,* and, selectively, the *Weekly Compilation of Presidential Documents. PAIS* is cumulated quarterly and annually and is available on CD-ROM and as an online database.

Reader's Guide to Periodical Literature. New York: H. W. Wilson, 1905—.
Articles in popular periodicals published in the United States are indexed by author and by subject in this semimonthly guide. Each yearly cumulation includes hundreds of citations about the presidency. The *Reader's Guide* is a vital reference tool for researching events within the past year. It is available as a CD-ROM product and as an online database.

Social Sciences Citation Index (SSCI). Philadelphia: Institute for Science Information, 1973—.
The Social Science Citation Index indexes a larger number of journals than any other index in the social sciences. The cited works include books, journal articles, dissertations, reports, proceedings, among others. There are four separate indexes: a source (author) index, a citation index, a corporate index, and a key word subject index. Items appearing in the citation index have been cited in footnotes or bibliographies in the social sciences. This index has several unique features that are helpful for studying the presidency. By using the corporate index, you can identify publications issued by particular organizations, such as the Brookings Institution. The source and citation indexes can be used to identify the writings of a particular scholar who has written extensively on the presidency, and to identify other researchers who have cited these writings. *SSCI* is published three times a year and cumulated annually. It is available on CD-ROM and as an online database.

Social Sciences Index. New York: H. W. Wilson, 1975—.
This quarterly work indexes articles found in most of the major social science journals, covering all of the major journals in political science. Every literature search on the presidency should

include this index. It is available on CD-ROM and as an online database.

Sociological Abstracts. San Diego, CA: Sociological Abstracts, 1952—.
This is the major abstracting service in the field of sociology. In addition to journals, it indexes papers presented at meetings and book reviews. The entries are arranged in thirty-three major categories. The author and subject indexes are cumulated annually. The service is available on CD-ROM and as an online database.

U.S. Government Periodicals Index. Bethesda, MD: Congressional Information Service, 1994—.
This quarterly index covers journals published by the federal government. The first issue of the print index was published in 1994 and covered journals published from October to December 1993. Access is by subject and author. Retrospective annual volumes will provide retrospective coverage to 1988. It is available on CD-ROM.

United States Political Science Documents. Pittsburgh: University Center for International Studies, University of Pittsburgh, 1976—.
The major U.S. political science journals are indexed and abstracted in this annual two-volume work. The first volume contains indexes by author, subject, geographic area, proper name, and journal title. The second volume abstracts the articles indexed in the first volume. This is another index that should be used in every search strategy. It is available as an online database.

Compact Disk Products

Many reference sources are now being published in the compact disk (CD-ROM) format. Printed indexes previously cited that are now in compact disk format are listed below.

ABC POL SCI on Disc.
This database corresponds to the printed *ABC POL SCI*. It indexes all of the major political science journals. Coverage is from 1984 to the present.

America: History and Life on Disc.
This database corresponds to the printed *America: History and Life*. It indexes journal articles, book reviews, and dissertations. Coverage is from 1984 to the present.

Humanities Index.
> This database corresponds to the printed *Humanities Index*. English-language periodicals in history, philosophy, and religion are indexed. Coverage is from 1984 to the present.

Index to Legal Periodicals.
> This database corresponds to the printed *Index to Legal Periodicals*. It indexes legal periodicals, yearbooks, and law reviews. Coverage is from 1981 to the present.

International Political Science Abstracts.
> This database corresponds to the printed *International Political Science Abstracts*. It includes major journals in political science, public law, international law, and international relations. Coverage is from 1989 to the present.

LegalTrac.
> This database contains citations to the major law periodicals and to some legal newspapers. Coverage is from 1980 to the present.

PAIS International.
> This product includes the *Public Affairs Information Service Bulletin*, which covers publications in public policy, economics, political science, and the social sciences. Coverage is from 1972 to the present.

Reader's Guide to Periodical Literature.
> This database, which corresponds to the printed version, indexes general interest magazines and some scholarly journals. Coverage is from 1983 to the present.

Social Sciences Citation Index Compact Disc Edition.
> This is a CD-ROM version of the printed *Social Sciences Citation Index (SSCI)*. This product indexes more social science journals than any other single index or CD-ROM product. Coverage is from 1981 to the present.

Social Sciences Index.
> This CD-ROM version of *Social Sciences Index* indexes English-language periodicals in the social sciences. Coverage is from 1983 to the present.

SocioFile.
> This CD-ROM subset of *Sociological Abstracts* provides abstracts from all of the major journals in sociology. Coverage is from 1974 to the present.

U.S. Government Periodicals Index.
> This database was published in 1994 and corresponds to the printed *U.S. Government Periodicals Index*. Retrospective coverage to 1988 will be included on future disks.

Another CD-ROM product that is of special interest to students of the presidency is called InfoTrac. InfoTrac is updated quarterly and provides citations to articles from general interest periodicals as well as some scholarly periodicals. For example, it indexes *Congress and the President*, the *National Journal*, and *Presidential Studies Quarterly*. It also indexes the *Weekly Compilation of Presidential Documents* and the *Congressional Quarterly Weekly Report*. Many of the journals indexed on InfoTrac are now available with the full text of the articles.

In addition, there are three CD-ROM products, Government Publications Index on InfoTrac, Government Documents Catalog Subscription Service, and GPO on Silver Platter, that can be used for identifying U.S. government publications, including those related to the study of the presidency.

Databases

Online databases are extremely useful because they retrieve information quickly. The following online services are especially helpful to scholars of the presidency and can be used in a variety of ways, such as obtaining information on presidential actions, speeches, and vetoes; providing background information; and displaying many presidential documents in their entirety. A new text on online legal research by Christopher G. Wren and Jill Robinson Wren is especially useful for learning how to search two of the online services. Published in 1994 by Adams and Ambrose, the book is entitled *Using Computers in Legal Research: A Guide to LEXIS and WESTLAW*.

CQ's WASHINGTON ALERT. Washington, DC: Congressional Quarterly.
> This congressional tracking service provides the full text of each version of a bill or resolution, summaries of bills and resolutions prepared by the Congressional Research Service, full texts of

committee and conference reports, full texts of the *Congressional Record*, committee and floor schedules, committee and subcommittee action, votes, rosters, and roll call votes. The full text of the *Congressional Quarterly Weekly Report* is available as is information from other Congressional Quarterly publications, including news from *CQ's Congressional Monitor*, the *CQ Fax Report*, *Politics in America*, and the *CQ Researcher*.

LEGI-SLATE. Washington, DC: LEGI-SLATE.
This database tracks and updates regulatory, congressional, and presidential activity and provides the full text of the *Federal Register* and the *Congressional Record*. Included are updates of committee schedules and congressional votes. There is also a news service with articles from the *National Journal* and the *Washington Post*.

LEXIS/NEXIS. Dayton, OH: Reed Elsevier Inc.
This database includes analyses from news transcripts such as CNN, ABC, and NPR and provides information from a variety of sources including the *National Journal* and the *Almanac of American Politics*. Numerous legal journals can also be accessed on LEXIS/NEXIS.

WESTLAW. St. Paul, MN: West Publishing Co.
This database can be used most effectively for finding citations related to the interpretation of public laws. It includes access to case law, statutes, administrative materials, and legal periodicals as well as access to other commercial databases. West publishes a *Westlaw Database List*, which describes the various databases that comprise WESTLAW.

All of these online services are expensive, so be sure to check to see whether your library provides access to them for a fee or at no charge. Also, if you are interested in any of the indexes listed earlier that are available online, check with a nearby library regarding cost and availability.

Journals

While scholarly discussions about the presidency can be found in many journals, there are several that regularly contain articles about some aspect of presidential politics. Those journals are the *American Journal of Political Science*, the *American Political Science Review*, the *American Politics Quarterly*, the *Journal of Politics*, *Political Research Quarterly*, and *Polity*.

In addition, the four journals listed below deserve special mention, as they all focus on the presidency.

Congress and the Presidency: A Journal of Capitol Studies. Washington, DC: Center for Congressional and Presidential Studies, American University, 1983—.
This journal covers both Congress and the presidency, focusing on the interaction between the two and on national policymaking in general. Published twice a year, it contains a mix of articles from political science and history. It also includes research notes, review essays, and book reviews.

Congressional Quarterly Weekly Report. Washington, DC: Congressional Quarterly, 1945—.
This journal recounts the important congressional activities of the previous week, including developments in committees as well as on the floor. When covering major pieces of legislation, it often provides voting records. Lobbying activities are given considerable coverage, with special reports on the relationship between congressional voting and interest groups. Each issue usually contains several articles on special issues or major legislation pending in Congress. The journal also contains a great deal of information useful for researching the presidency. Congressional Quarterly indexes the *Weekly Report* both quarterly and annually. The *Weekly Report* is also indexed in the *Public Affairs Information Service Bulletin* and in the *Social Sciences Index*. The *Weekly Report* is available online through CQ's WASHINGTON ALERT and DATATIMES.

National Journal: The Weekly on Politics and Government. Washington, DC: National Journal, 1969—.
The *National Journal* covers all areas of the federal government. It provides excellent analyses of the activities of the president. Each issue usually contains two or more feature articles on some aspect of presidential politics. At the end of the issue there is a detailed index for that issue, as well as a cumulative index for recent weeks. The *National Journal* is self-indexed by subject semi-annually and is also indexed in the *Public Affairs Information Service Bulletin*. It is available online through LEXIS/NEXIS and LEGI-SLATE.

Presidential Studies Quarterly. New York: Center for the Study of the Presidency, 1972—.
This journal focuses solely on the presidency. It regularly includes ten or more feature articles addressing a single theme. While

most of the articles are written by historians or political scientists, it does include articles from other fields. In addition, current and former political officials contribute articles. A lengthy book review section is provided as well.

Newsmagazines

Newsmagazines are an excellent source of current information about the presidency. They include news stories, editorials, and feature articles on the presidency. The magazines listed below regularly carry articles on the presidency that are written from a variety of political viewpoints. The best indexes to use for finding articles from newsmagazines are the *Reader's Guide to Periodical Literature* and InfoTrac. Many of these magazines are available on various online services, such as LEXIS/NEXIS, CQ's WASHINGTON ALERT, LEGI-SLATE, and WESTLAW. Since the online services change what they carry, the best way to determine what magazines are available is to check online. These newsmagazines are most useful for keeping up on current events and as a record of public opinion via their editorials and opinion articles.

Atlantic Monthly. Boston: Atlantic Monthly Company, 1857—.

CQ Researcher. Washington, DC: Congressional Quarterly, 1991—.

Commentary. New York: American Jewish Committee, 1945—.

Common Cause Magazine. Washington, DC: Common Cause, 1983—.

Current. Washington, DC: Heldref Publications, 1960—.

Harper's Magazine. New York: Harper's Magazine Company, 1851—.

Human Events: The National Conservative Weekly. Washington, DC: Human Events, 1944—.

National Review: A Journal of Fact and Opinion. New York: National Review, 1955—.

New Republic: A Journal of Opinion. Washington, DC: New Republic, 1914—.

Newsweek. New York: Newsweek, 1933—.

Progressive. Madison, WI: Progressive, 1909—.

Society: Social Science and Modern Society. New Brunswick, NJ: Transactions Periodicals Consortium, Rutgers University, 1963—.

Time: The Weekly Newsmagazine. New York: Time-Life, 1923—.

U.S. News and World Report. Washington, DC: U.S. News and World Report, 1933—.

Washington Monthly. Washington, DC: Washington Monthly Company, 1969—.

Newspapers and Indexes

The two best newspapers for following the presidency are *The New York Times* and the *Washington Post*. UMI (University Microfilms) has put full text versions of *The New York Times* and the *Washington Post* on CD-ROM starting with 1990. They call these versions NYT on Disc and Washington Post on Disc. The *National Newspaper Index* indexes *The New York Times*, the *Washington Post*, and other major newspapers. This microfilm index is cumulative and updated regularly. The *National Newspaper Index* is also available on CD-ROM.

Another online database is DATATIMES, which indexes both U.S. and international newspapers, news services, and business journals. Especially useful is its indexing of the *Washington Post* and the *Congressional Quarterly Weekly Report*. The *NewsBank Index* indexes selected articles from more than 450 U.S. newspapers, beginning in January 1982. The full text of articles is available on microfiche. The CD-ROM version of this index is called CD Newsbank. It is also available as an online database service.

Finally, you should also remember to check the online services, LEXIS/NEXIS, CQ's WASHINGTON ALERT, WESTLAW, and LEGI-SLATE, to see which newspapers are available there. For example, LEXIS/NEXIS carries *The New York Times* and the *Washington Post* as well as numerous other newspapers.

News Services

The online databases CQ's WASHINGTON ALERT, LEXIS/NEXIS, LEGI-SLATE, and WESTLAW the best way to locate the most recent information. These online services offer the transcripts of television and radio news broadcasts and many other sources of news and analyses from the previous day. However, if you do not have access to any of the online databases, then news services can be most useful since they are only a week or two behind the events in their publication.

Facts on File (New York: Facts on File, 1940—) is another printed source that provides information about very recent events. *Facts on File* is a weekly digest of world events, but the emphasis is on the United States. The entries are grouped under broad topics, such as world affairs or national affairs. There is a cumulative index. A CD-ROM entitled FACTS ON FILE NEWS DIGEST is available.

A new product published by Research Publications International is Broadcast News on CD-ROM. It offers transcripts of more than seventy television and radio news broadcasts from ABC, CNN, PBS, NPR, and other news programs. It is updated every month and can be tailored to include only specific stations.

Statistical Sources

In addition to finding data about election returns, students and researchers can find data about a variety of other presidential activities. In addition to the work described below, you should also refer to the factbooks cited earlier.

Ragsdale, Lyn. *Vital Statistics on the Presidency: Washington to Clinton.* Washington, DC: CQ Press, 1995.
This statistical handbook covers the personal backgrounds of the presidents, presidential selection and elections, public opinion, public appearances, presidential policy decisions, presidential bureaucracy, presidential relations with Congress, and presidential relations with the courts. There are over 150 tables and figures that summarize and illustrate aspects of both the individual presidents and the presidency as an institution.

Primary Sources and Finding Tools

Researching the Presidency

In this chapter we will examine the primary tools for finding presidential documents. We will also discuss how to access sources of information about press conferences, vetoes, elections, and other aspects of the presidency.

Doing research on the presidency means you must be familiar with all of the branches of government and know how to identify the documents issued by each. Legal research is the analysis of legal decisionmaking, including the rules, laws, and decisions formulated by the executive, legislative, and judicial branches of government. In this chapter we discuss three kinds of primary legal sources: administrative law, statutory law, and case law. We also describe the finding tools needed to identify specific rules, laws, and cases.

Administrative law is comprised of the rules and orders that interpret statutory law issued by the president, executive departments, administrative agencies, and regulatory commissions. Knowing which finding tools will help you identify, update, and interpret these rules and regulations is essential for anyone researching the presidency. Statutory law is the written law enacted by Congress. As a bill passes through Congress, various legislative documents are generated. These documents, which make up a bill's legislative history, are frequently used in legal argument because they show the legislative intent of a statute. It is important that you know how to compile a legislative history. Case law is the law as defined by previously decided cases. The researcher must know how to identify and analyze the decisions, oral arguments, and opinions associated with the Supreme Court. After identifying all of the necessary primary and secondary sources, the researcher can proceed to analyze the accumulated material.

Research Guides to Government Publications

The following guides, with the most recently published listed first, are the best guides to current government and legal sources. They describe how to find and use government publications and legal finding tools. Most are available in college, university, or public libraries.

Lowery, Roger C., and Sue A. Cody. *Political Science: Illustrated Search Strategy and Sources with an Introduction to Legal Research for Undergraduates.* Ann Arbor, MI: Pierian Press, 1993.
    This is an excellent guide for students working in the field of political science. The volume includes a good introduction on how to choose a topic and how to find books, articles, and other basic sources. An excellent chapter on locating U.S. government documents and a detailed chapter on doing legal research are very useful. This well-organized work presents difficult material in an easy-to-understand format, employing numerous illustrations and charts.

Morehead, Joe, and Mary Fetzer. *Introduction to United States Government Information Sources.* 4th ed. Englewood, CO: Libraries Unlimited, 1992.
    This is a valuable guide for anyone interested in researching federal documents. The chapter on the presidency contains a wealth of information. There are also separate chapters on the legislative branch, executive departments, independent agencies, and the judiciary. The book has useful information on how the depository library system operates and on the work of the Government Printing Office and the Superintendent of Documents. This volume provides an excellent explanation of the technical aspects of documents, such as the SuDocs classification system.

Cohen, Morris L. *Legal Research in a Nutshell.* 5th ed. St. Paul, MN: West Publishing Co., 1992.
    This is an excellent short guide to legal research. It includes chapters on administrative law, statutes, legislative histories, and other aspects of the law. While detailed, it is easy to comprehend. Both the beginner and the skilled researcher will find it valuable.

Jacobstein, J. Myron, and Roy M. Mersky. *Fundamentals of Legal Research.* 5th ed. Westbury, NY: Foundation Press, 1990.
    This is a basic text for students learning to do legal research. Those interested in the presidency will find useful the discussion

and explanation of federal legislation and federal legislative histories. A glossary of legal terms and a table of legal abbreviations are included.

Goehlert, Robert U., and Fenton S. Martin. *The Presidency: A Research Guide.* 2d ed. Santa Barbara, CA: ABC-Clio, 1985.
This volume details how to research the presidency using both federal and commercial resources. It also offers a lengthy discussion of the secondary sources used in researching the presidency, including campaigns and elections. It identifies the relevant dictionaries, encyclopedias, newsmagazines, newsletters, bibliographies, journals, and indexes and provides information on finding statistics, archival material, oral histories, television transcripts, and biographical material.

Guides to the Presidency

Guides are an excellent starting point for the researcher seeking to answer a specific question or desiring an overview of some aspect of the presidency.

Edwards, George C., and Stephen J. Wayne. *Studying the Presidency.* Knoxville: University of Tennessee Press, 1983.
The first part of this guide deals with approaches, cases, concepts, and analyses used in the study of the presidency. The second part describes sources employed in researching presidential studies. These include indexes, congressional documents, legal documents, and presidential libraries. The last two chapters of the book discuss interviewing presidential aides.

Guide to the Presidency. 2d ed. Washington, DC: Congressional Quarterly, 1996.
This is the best single volume reference work on the presidency, able to answer most general reference questions. It begins with an account of the origins and history of the presidency and includes chapters on executive powers and presidential relations with the other branches of government. This volume is most valuable to the researcher who is seeking a basic, yet thorough understanding of the presidency.

Presidential Publications

The term *presidential papers* encompasses all of the material associated with a president. It includes the papers under the control of the executive office (for example, interdepartmental reports), official papers (often referred to as the "private papers" or "White House papers"), and personal papers (for example, letters). The government does not publish the papers that are under the control of the executive office. These are passed on to succeeding administrations. Some of this material is available, however, because a president has released it or because it has come to light under the Freedom of Information Act, a congressional investigation, or a court decision. Neither does the government publish papers considered to be the president's personal property. Much of this can be found in the Library of Congress and in presidential libraries. Access to these materials will be discussed later.

In the following sections, we will detail the kinds of materials contained in the public papers of a president. We will then describe how to use a variety of government and commercial reference tools to identify them.

Legislative and Administrative Papers

Under statutory law, Congress has authorized the president to take certain actions expressed as executive orders and proclamations. Executive orders are claimed by virtue of the office, by the power authorized under the Constitution, as commander-in-chief, or under statutory law. They have the effect of law. Though never defined by statute, any act of the president authorizing an action is an executive order. While executive orders can deal with a wide variety of matters, they generally relate to the conduct of government business and the organization and procedures of the executive branch. For example, reorganization plans are essentially presidential orders. Issued under prior congressional authority, they enable the president to change the structure of the executive branch by combining, abolishing, or switching agencies under the level of department.

There is no legal distinction between an executive order and a proclamation, but not all proclamations have the effect of law. For example, a call for a public observance does not have the force of law. Proclamations are issued by virtue of the office, existing laws, or as a response to a joint resolution and are generally issued for matters of widespread interest. Proclamations and executive orders can overlap in content.

Foreign Affairs

Treaties and executive agreements are issued under the power of the Constitution and existing legislation. A treaty is a compact with a foreign nation made by the president and approved by two-thirds of the Senate. Treaties are also referred to as conventions, contracts, or protocols.

Executive agreements are made by the president under the constitutional authority invested in the president as the chief executive and under existing legislation. In contrast to treaties, they do not require the approval of the Senate.

Messages

Presidential messages include all communications made to the Congress, whether written or oral. Most, though not all of these messages are published by Congress. Messages can be divided into several categories.

The first category refers to messages conveyed when approving or vetoing a bill. The Constitution states that "every Bill which shall have passed the House of Representatives and the Senate, shall, before it becomes a Law, be presented to the President of the United States." Though the only constitutional requirement is that the bill be signed, a president may include a message as well. If a president does not sign a bill, then "he shall return it, with his Objections to that House in which it shall have originated." A veto is a presidential message as well as an important type of executive power.

The second category refers to presidential addresses before the Congress. The annual State of the Union Address is an example of such an address. The president's addresses need not be made on a regular basis. They are more likely to be given upon a special occasion. Also included in this category are documents that the president is required to submit to Congress.

The last category is comprised of speeches made by the president on television, radio, or before official and unofficial gatherings. It also includes press conferences, press releases, and other miscellaneous materials issued officially.

Textual Sources

Now that we have discussed the various kinds of presidential documents, we will identify sources that can be used to find presidential publications. As we will not discuss every source, especially those best suited for retrospective materials, be sure to check the guides to government publications listed earlier, or ask librarians for additional sources.

Bevans, Charles I. *Treaties and Other International Agreements of the United States of America 1776–1949*. Washington, DC: U.S. Government Printing Office, 1968—.
This compilation contains all of the treaty and agreement texts prior to 1950. Each volume has an index, and there are cumulative

analytical indexes. Commonly referred to as "Bevans," this is the
most comprehensive collection of treaties available.

Compilation of Messages and Papers of the Presidents, 1789–1927. 20 vols. Ed.
James D. Richardson. New York: Bureau of National Literature, 1928.
This work is an unofficial compilation of presidential papers and
materials from Washington to Coolidge. It includes the texts of
presidential proclamations, addresses, annual messages, veto
messages, and other communications to Congress.

Congressional Record: Proceedings and Debates of the Congress. Washington,
DC: U.S. Government Printing Office, 1873—.
This offers a daily record of the proceedings of the House and
Senate, the extensions (written submissions and remarks), and
the Daily Digest. It offers a history of legislation as well. The pro-
ceedings are indexed by subject and name. The *Congressional
Record* is an important tool for finding presidential messages and
communications to Congress, roll call votes, and congressional
action on vetoed bills. Prior to the publication of the *Congressional
Record*, the floor proceedings were published in the *Annals of
Congress*, the *Register of Debates in Congress*, and the *Congressional
Globe*. The *Congressional Record* is available online through
CQ's WASHINGTON ALERT, LEXIS/NEXIS, LEGI-SLATE, and
WESTLAW. The full text of the *Congressional Record* is available
on the Internet through GPO ACCESS and THOMAS.

Department of State Bulletin. Washington, DC: U.S. Government Printing
Office, 1939—.
From 1939 to 1977 the *Bulletin* was a weekly publication with
semi-annual indexes. Since then it has been issued monthly with
an annual index. As the official record of foreign policy, it is an
invaluable tool for studying treaties. Documents included in the
Bulletin are presidential addresses, remarks, radio and television
excerpts, correspondence and memoranda, exchanges and greet-
ings with foreign dignitaries and official joint communiqués,
messages and reports to Congress, and news conferences and
proclamations relating to foreign affairs. The annual index lists
these materials under the entry, "Presidential Documents." There
are also sections in each issue devoted to treaty ratifications and
announcements of executive agreements. In addition to its own
index, the *Bulletin* is also indexed in *Public Affairs Information Service Bulletin*, the *Index to U.S. Government Periodicals*, and *Reader's
Guide to Periodical Literature*.

Federal Register. Washington, DC: U.S. National Archives and Records Service, 1936—.

Code of Federal Regulations. Washington, DC: U.S. National Archives and Records Service, 1949—.
These resources include executive orders, reorganization plans, and presidential proclamations of legal significance. Presidential executive orders and proclamations have been published in the *Federal Register* since 1936. *Title 3 of the Code of Federal Regulations* is a compilation of presidential documents, including a codification of presidential executive orders and proclamations by subject. The full text of the *Federal Register* is available starting with 1994 on the Internet through GPO ACCESS.

Public Papers of the Presidents of the United States. Washington, DC: U.S. Government Printing Office, 1958—.
Published annually, these volumes include oral and written statements by the president, communications to Congress, public speeches, press conferences, public letters, messages to heads of state, and executive documents. Bernam Press and Kraus International Publications have published the *Cumulated Indexes to the Public Papers of the Presidents.* The present ten-volume set includes indexes for Hoover, Truman, Eisenhower, Kennedy, Johnson, Nixon, Ford, Reagan, and Bush. Each volume indexes the complete public papers of a president into one alphabetical listing, covering the entire administration of that president.

TIARA CD-ROM: Treaties and International Agreements Researchers' Archive. Dobbs Ferry, NY: Oceana, 1993—.
This database contains the full text of all treaties to which the United States is a signatory from 1783 to the present. It can be searched by title, country, signatories, date signed, date-in-force, signing location, and subject. It also includes original charts and tables and any Senate reservations.

Treaties and Other International Acts Series. Washington, DC: U.S. Government Printing Office, 1945—.
This series, referred to as *TIAS,* is a continuation of the *Treaty Series,* which covers the years 1908–1945, and the *Executive Agreement Series,* which covers the years 1929–1945. The serially numbered treaties and agreements begin with the number 1501. Each text is published separately in pamphlet form six to twelve months after the treaty or act is in force. The text, printed both in English and the language of the other country involved, includes

important dates, presidential proclamations, and correspondence pertaining to the treaty or act.

U.S. Code Congressional and Administrative News. St. Paul, MN: West Publishing Co., 1939—.
This resource includes selected presidential messages, executive orders, and proclamations. Many presidential messages and re-organization plans are published separately as House and Senate documents. Reprints of the full text of all public laws and selected House and Senate documents and committee reports are published monthly. Information on statutes of legislation is available as well. One particularly helpful table provides a legislative history of all bills passed into law. This cumulative series is an excellent tool for legislative tracing.

United States Treaties and Other International Agreements. Washington, DC: U.S. Government Printing Office, 1950—.
This annual publication, referred to as *UST,* provides the text of treaties and agreements proclaimed during the preceding year in the language of the original instrument. It contains a subject and country index. Prior to 1950 the treaties and agreements were published in the *United States Statutes at Large. UST* cumulates and replaces the *Treaties and Other International Acts Series (TIAS).*

Weekly Compilation of Presidential Documents. Washington, DC: U.S. National Archives and Records Service, 1965—.
This resource includes messages, statements, public speeches, remarks, press conferences, and other material released by the White House. It is published every Monday to cover the activities of the preceding week. Some speeches and press releases are available on the Internet through the White House home page on the World Wide Web.

Indexes to Texts

In the previous section we described a variety of finding tools that contain different kinds of presidential documents. Many of the bibliographical tools cited are both an index to presidential actions and an index and compilation of the documents themselves. The following items are additional indexes to texts and presidential activities that do not include any texts.

American Foreign Policy Index. Bethesda, MD: Congressional Information Service, 1993—.
This quarterly index covers unclassified government documents dealing with foreign affairs. This includes periodicals, monographs, serials, press briefings, treaty documents, speeches, congressional reports, hearings, handbooks, and research papers. It is published in two sections, an index and corresponding abstract section. Information is indexed by subject, personal name, geographic area, issuing source, bill number, and publication title and number.

CIS Federal Register Index. Bethesda, MD: Congressional Information Service, 1984—.
This weekly index contains three parts: an index by subject and name providing access by subject, geographical area, issuing agency, industry, corporation, organization, individual name, and legislation; an index by *Code of Federal Regulations* section number specifying when and where final or proposed changes to the *Code* have been announced; and an index by agency docket number. Each index entry provides the issuing agency, register issue date, type of document, and *Federal Register* page number.

CIS/Index: Congressional Information Service/Index to Publications of the United States Congress. Washington, DC: Congressional Information Service, 1970—.
This is an inclusive monthly index to all congressional publications. It abstracts every form of publication emanating from the legislative process. Materials are indexed by subject, name, committee, bill number, report number, document number, and name of committee chair. Because *CIS/Index* abstracts reports, hearings, and other congressional documents, the researcher can save valuable time by reading the synopses of publications. For most researchers, *CIS/Index* should be the first place to look when tracing legislation.

Since 1984, *CIS* has published a *CIS Legislative Histories Annual*, showing exactly what items are included in a law's history, full citations for the publications in the law's history, concise annotations of the publications, and a summary of the law's purpose. There are quarterly cumulative indexes, and at the end of the year the *CIS/Annual* is issued. There is also the *CIS Five-Year Cumulative Index 1970–1974*, the *CIS Four-Year Cumulative Index 1975–1978*, the *CIS Four-Year Cumulative Index 1979–1982*, and the *CIS Four-Year Cumulative Index 1983–1986*, the *CIS Four-Year Cumulative Index 1987–1990*, and the *CIS Four-Year Cumulative Index 1991–1994*.

CIS/Index is available on CD-ROM as Congressional Masterfile II, which indexes congressional documents appearing in the printed *CIS/Index* since 1970. This includes hearings, committee prints, reports, and documents. Congressional Masterfile II also includes *Reports Required by Congress: CIS Guide to Executive Communications.* Congressional Masterfile I provides retrospective indexing to congressional hearings and prints to 1789.

CIS Index to Presidential Executive Orders and Proclamations. Bethesda, MD: Congressional Information Service, 1987.
This two-part index covers presidential documents issued between 1789 and 1983. The set is published in two chronological parts: Washington through Wilson (1789–1921) and Harding into Reagan's first term (1921–1983). There are five separate finding aids: an index by subject and organization, an index by personal name, a chronological list of all numbered and unnumbered orders and proclamations, an index of interrelated orders and proclamations, and an index by site and document number that allows researchers to locate items by agency, assigned geographical site, or document number. The *CIS Federal Register Index* provides access to executive orders and proclamations issued after 1983.

Monthly Catalog of United States Government Publications. Washington, DC: U.S. Government Printing Office, 1895—.
This is an important index for identifying presidential messages and treaty documents. The *Monthly Catalog* has a subject index and an index arranged by government author. A CD-ROM version of the *Monthly Catalog,* called Government Documents Catalog Subscription Services (GDCS), covers the period from 1976 to the present. It can be searched by author, title, subject, SuDocs number, and report number. It is much more efficient to use the GDCS than the printed *Monthly Catalog.*

Treaties in Force. Washington, DC: U.S. Government Printing Office, 1929–.
This annual publication, referred to as *TIF,* lists treaties and agreements of the United States that are in effect. The first part lists bilateral treaties and other agreements by country and then by topic. The second part lists multinational agreements by subject and then by country. The series also cites supersedings and terminations of treaty articles and identifies amendments and supplementary treaties. The *Department of State Bulletin* provides a monthly update.

United States Statutes at Large: Containing the Laws and Concurrent Resolutions Enacted. . . . Washington, DC: U.S. Government Printing Office, 1789—.

The *Statutes at Large* is a record of all laws published in their final form, giving the full text of congressional acts and resolutions passed during a congressional session. Slip laws—the texts of individual acts—are published separately as they are passed and contain legislative histories on their inside back covers. These are indexed in the *Monthly Catalog*. The *Statutes at Large* also includes the text of proclamations. It can be used as an index to presidential messages to Congress.

The following outline lists reference tools for identifying presidential publications that are useful for doing preliminary research and for finding background information and citations to documentary matter. Some of the tools listed for finding current materials can also be used for retrospective searching, since many of them have been published over a considerable period of time. The outline emphasizes current research. Consequently, we have not fully described tools useful only for historical research, especially guides to documents of the eighteenth and nineteenth centuries. Be sure to check the guides to government publications listed earlier or ask a librarian for additional reference tools.

A complete collection of documents about a presidential activity would include the following:

1. A history of related presidential activities and publications prior and subsequent to the event in question.

2. Materials from executive departments and regulatory agencies concerning the event.

3. Materials from special interest groups regarding the event.

4. Congressional publications from the legislative process and statements from legislators regarding the event.

5. Any relevant court cases and decisions that relate to the event.

6. Useful secondary analysis and histories, including journal and newspaper articles. These can be identified using indexes, CD-ROMs, or online databases, as well as material from:
    National Journal
    CQ Weekly Report
    Washington Post
    The New York Times

7. A search of online information services for background information as well as information and documents about the presidential action itself. This would include search on:

> CQ's WASHINGTON ALERT
> LEGI-SLATE
> LEXIS/NEXIS
> WESTLAW

8. A search on the Internet for background information as well as for actual presidential documents of all kinds and information regarding presidential activities. This would include using:

> White House Home Page (*http://www.whitehouse.gov/*)
> THOMAS (*http://thomas.loc.gov*)
> MARVEL (*gopher://marvel.loc.gov*)
> GPO ACCESS (*http://www.access.gpo.gov*)

9. Information regarding presidential action—that is, the signing or vetoing of a bill—can be found using the following finding tools:

   a. For the text of statements go to

   > *Congressional Record*
   > *Congressional Quarterly Weekly Report*
   > *Weekly Compilation of Presidential Documents*
   > *Public Papers of the President*

   b. For references to the text go to

   > *Congressional Record Index*
   > *CIS/Index*
   > *Monthly Catalog*
   > *Statutes at Large*

10. Information regarding proclamations and executive orders can be found using the following finding tools:

    a. For the text go to

    > *U.S. Code Congressional and Administrative News*
    > *Federal Register*
    > *Title 3 CFR*
    > *Public Papers of the Presidents*
    > *CQ Almanac*
    > *Compilation of the Messages and Papers of the President 1789–1897*

    b. For references to the text go to

    > *CIS Federal Register Index*

CIS Presidential Orders and Proclamations
Code of Federal Regulations, Title 3
Federal Register Index

11. Information regarding presidential messages to Congress can be found using the following finding tools:

    a. For the text of messages to Congress go to
        Weekly Compilation of Presidential Documents
        Congressional Record
        Congressional Quarterly Weekly Report
        CQ Almanac
        U.S. Code Congressional and Administrative News
        Public Papers of the Presidents
        Compilation of the Messages and Papers of the President 1789–1897

    b. For references to messages to Congress go to
        Cumulative indexes in the *Weekly Compilation of Presidential Documents*
        Congressional Record Index
        CIS/Index
        Monthly Catalog
        Public Affairs Information Service Bulletin
        Statutes at Large

12. Information regarding presidential messages to the public (for example, televized speeches, radio addresses, press conferences, press releases, addresses before groups) can be found using the following finding tools:

    a. For the text of public messages go to
        Weekly Compilation of Presidential Documents
        Congressional Quarterly Weekly Report
        CQ Almanac
        Newspapers
        Public Papers of the Presidents

    b. For references to the text of public messages go to
        Cumulative indexes in the *Weekly Compilation of Presidential Documents*
        Monthly Catalog
        Public Affairs Information Service Bulletin
        Newspaper indexes

13. Information regarding treaties can be found using the following finding tools:

a. For the text of treaties go to
 Department of State Bulletin
 TIARA CD-ROM: Treaties and International Agreements
  Researchers' Archive
 Treaties and Other International Acts Series (TIAS)
 U.S. Treaties and Other International Agreements (UST)
 *Treaties and Other International Agreements of the United States
  of America* (Bevans)

b. For references to the text of treaties go to
 Congressional Index
 CIS/Index
 Monthly Catalog
 Treaties in Force
 American Foreign Policy Index

Access to resources can vary, so you will need to change or modify this outline to suit your needs, taking into consideration which print and electronic sources are available to you.

Information Sources on the Presidency

In addition to presidential publications directly related to the presidency, there are many other finding tools that can be used to identify primary and secondary sources about the presidency. Examples are press conferences, vetoes, and election returns, among others.

Speeches and Press Conferences

Speeches and press conferences are the primary methods of presidential communication to the public. Listed below are a variety of reference tools for locating speeches and press conferences. In addition to the sources listed here, you should also check online database services, newspaper indexes, the *Reader's Guide to Periodical Literature*, the *Congressional Quarterly Weekly Report*, *Facts on File*, and many of the sources already mentioned in the preceding sections. Don't forget to check the Internet where many presidential speeches and press releases are available.

Vital Speeches of the Day. New York: City News Publishing Co., 1934—.
 This monthly journal prints important speeches of U.S. leaders verbatim. In addition to presidential speeches, you can find speeches by other members of the executive office, including

members of the Council of Economic Advisors, the National Security Council, and policy advisors.

White House Weekly. Washington, DC: Feistritzer Publications, 1981—. This publication offers a weekly analysis of the president. It focuses on the president's schedule, statements, speeches, and style and is indexed quarterly.

The following items provide quick reference to inaugural addresses, State of the Union addresses, and major campaign speeches.

Israel, Fred L., ed. *The State of the Union Messages of Presidents 1790–1966.* 3 vols. New York: Chelsea House, 1966.

Lott, Davis N. *The Presidents Speak: The Inaugural Addresses of American Presidents from Washington to Clinton.* New York: Holt, 1994.

Podell, Janet, and Steven Anzovin. *Speeches of the American Presidents.* New York: H. W. Wilson, 1988.

Ryan, Halford. *Inaugural Addresses of Twentieth-Century American Presidents.* Westport, CT: Greenwood Press, 1993.

Singer, Aaron, ed. *Campaign Speeches of American Presidential Candidates, 1928–1972.* New York: Frederick Ungar Publishing Co., 1976.

A very useful home page on the World Wide Web that provides presidential inaugural addresses and other selected addresses can be found at the following address: *(http://grid.let.rug.nl/~welling/usa/presidents/addresses.html)*.

There are several compilations of press conferences. In addition to the following volumes, you can use the *Weekly Compilation of Presidential Documents,* the *Public Papers of the Presidents,* online database services, and newspaper indexes to identify press conferences.

U.S. President Press Conferences. Washington, DC: Brookhave Press, 1971. This is a microfilm record of all of the press conferences of Woodrow Wilson, Calvin Coolidge, Herbert Hoover, Franklin D. Roosevelt, and Harry Truman (1913–1952). President Harding did not hold any press conferences.

The Johnson Presidential Press Conferences. Pine Plains, NY: Earl M. Coleman Enterprises, 1978.

The Kennedy Presidential Press Conferences. Pine Plains, NY: Earl M. Coleman Enterprises, 1978.

The Nixon Presidential Press Conferences. Pine Plains, NY: Earl M. Coleman
Enterprises, 1978.
These volumes arrange the press conference chronologically.
They are indexed and cross-indexed by subject and public figure
sections.

Vetoes

The following are useful tools for researching vetoes.

Presidential Vetoes, 1789–1988. Washington, DC: U.S. Government Printing
Office, 1992.

Presidential Vetoes, 1989–1991. Washington, DC: U.S. Government Printing
Office, 1992.
These two guides list all bills vetoed in chronological order, arranged by congressional session and presidential administration.
The vetoes are listed by bill number. The document number and
pages of the *Congressional Record* where the message is printed
are provided as well.

The single compilation of presidential vetoes is listed below. You can
find the message of presidential vetoes in the *Congressional Record*, the
Weekly Compilation of Presidential Documents, and the *Public Papers of the
President.*

U.S. Congress. Senate. *Veto Messages of the Presidents of the United States,
with the Action of Congress Thereon.* Compiled by Ben Perley Poore.
49th Cong., 2d Sess. S. Doc. 53, Washington, DC: U.S. Government
Printing Office, 1883.

Presidential Advisory Commissions

Advisory commissions and committees are established to assist the
president and are listed in the *U.S. Government Manual* in the section entitled "Guide to Boards, Committees and Commissions." These commissions and committees issue reports on their findings. Information on their
publication appears in the *Monthly Catalog* and on the CD-ROM index,
Government Documents Catalog Subscription Service. The publications
are indexed by key word, title, and subject. When the report of a presiden-

tial commission or committee is known under a popular name, its official title can be identified in *Popular Names of U.S. Government Reports: A Catalog*, which lists reports alphabetically under popular name. John Androit's *Guide to U.S. Government Publications* (McLean, VA: Documents Index, 1973–) includes names of commissions and committees in its index.

Information on presidential commissions and committees can be located in the following works.

Federal Advisory Committees, Annual Report of the President. Washington, DC: U.S. Government Printing Office, 1973—.
This annual report lists all of the advisory committees within the White House: the executive office of the president, departments, independent establishments, committees within committees, commissions, and councils. It is arranged alphabetically by title.

Federal Register. Washington, DC: U.S. Government Printing Office, 1936—.
The *Federal Register* publishes notices about the establishment of federal advisory committees and commissions. It also notes when their meetings are to take place.

Sullivan, Linda, ed. *Encyclopedia of Governmental Advisory Organizations*. Detroit: Gale Research Company, 1973—.
This work identifies committees, boards, councils, and other advisory groups serving the federal government. It provides the office name, popular name, telephone, address, dates, authority, membership, staff, activities, publications, and subsidiary units for each entry. There is a cumulative index by subject and name.

New Governmental Advisory Organizations. Detroit: Gale, 1976—.
This publication updates Gale's *Encyclopedia of Governmental Advisory Organizations*. It is issued periodically between editions of the *Encyclopedia*.

Zink, Steven P., comp. *Guide to Presidential Advisory Commissions, 1973–1984*. Alexandria, VA: Chadwyck-Healey, 1987.
This guide lists commissions and other ad hoc presidential advisory bodies established between 1972 and 1984. It contains a chronological listing of advisory commissions and provides identifying information for each, including the official and popular name of a commission; citations to published documents; a statement of the commissions' function; dates, places, and nature of meetings; availability of printed copies; and abstracts of issued reports.

Tollefson, Alan M., and H.C. Chang, eds. *A Bibliography of Presidential Commissions, Committees, Councils, Panels, and Task Forces, 1961–1972.* St. Paul: Government Publications Division, University of Minnesota Libraries, 1973.
This selective bibliography lists in alphabetical order 243 publications issued by advisory groups. There are indexes for personal name, title, and subject by key word.

Wolanin, Thomas R. *Presidential Advisory Commissions: Truman and Nixon.* Madison: University of Wisconsin Press, 1975.
This volume can be used to trace ad hoc advisory bodies from Truman to 1972.

Executive Office

The various offices of the executive office of the president provide another source of information about the activities of the presidency. In this section we will identify some of the major publications of the Office of Management and Budget, the Central Intelligence Agency, the National Security Council, and the Council of Economic Advisors. In general, the best tools for identifying publications of the executive office are the *Monthly Catalog*, the *CIS/Index*, the *American Foreign Policy Index*, and any of the CD-ROM indexes to documents (Government Documents Catalog Subscription Service, GPO on Silver Platter, and Government Publications Index on InfoTrac). *CIS/Index* is especially useful for finding testimony given before committees by individuals in the executive office, such as the director of the Office of Management and Budget and the chair of the Council of Economic Advisors. The *American Foreign Policy Index* indexes some publications from the Central Intelligence Agency, the Office of Management and Budget, and the National Security Council. There is also a considerable amount of information and actual documents from the executive branch available on the Internet. For example, the *Budget of the United States* appears on the Internet. The White House home page on the World Wide Web also has a section for the executive branch that can be used to find documents and background information.

The Office of Management and Budget (OMB) issues the following publications. All executive budget publications are noted in the *Weekly Compilation of Presidential Documents* and are indexed in the *Monthly Catalog* and the CD-ROM indexes.

The Budget of the United States Government. Washington, DC: U.S. Government Printing Office, 1972—.
This annual publication contains the president's message on the

budget. It summarizes his proposed plans for the budget and any recommended taxes.

The Budget of the United States Government, Appendix. Washington, DC: U.S. Government Printing Office, 1972—.
This annual publication accompanies the OMB publication entitled *The Budget of the United States Government*. It gives detailed estimates for the budget, arranged by agency and account. It is essentially a line item identification of the budget.

The U.S. Budget in Brief. Washington, DC: U.S. Government Printing Office, 1972—.
This is an abridged version of OMB's *Budget of the United States Government*. For rapid access to information on the budget, this publication is the one to consult.

The Central Intelligence Agency (CIA) publishes maps, atlases, reports, directories, and other analytic studies. There are no bibliographies, indexes, or catalogs that list all documents published by the CIA. The researcher may check the *Monthly Catalog* or any of the CD-ROM indexes to documents to ascertain what CIA documents have been made available. Many of the publications, such as directories, technical reports, journals, and dictionaries, are released by the Document Expediting Project (DOCEX) of the Library of Congress. You can also consult a publication of the National Foreign Assessment Center, *CIA Publications Released to the Public through Library of Congress DOCEX: Listing for 1972–1977*. Updates of this bibliography have also been published.

While most National Security Council (NSC) publications are still classified, some have been made available to the public. University Publications of America has collected many of these documents and published them as microfilm sets. Each set includes a printed guide.

Documents of the National Security Council, 1947–1977. Frederick, MD: University Publications of America, 1980. Microfilm.
In addition to this basic collection, six supplemental collections of NSC documents have been issued by University Publications of America as part of a continuing series. The publisher has also issued on microfilm three sets of *Minutes of Meeting of the National Security Council*.

The Council of Economic Advisors (CEA) consists of three members appointed by the president with congressional consent. They serve the president by providing economic advice based on analyses of the national economy and federal economic programs and assist in preparing the president's economic reports to Congress. They issue the following publications:

Economic Report of the President. Washington, DC: U.S. Government Printing Office, 1947—.
 This publication is the president's economic report to Congress and the annual report of the Council of Economic Advisors. It covers economic developments, trends, and recommendations.

International Economic Report of the President. Washington, DC: U.S. Government Printing Office, 1973—.
 This annual publication deals with the economic aspects of the United States in relation to the rest of the world.

Platforms

Both the Democratic and Republican parties publish a written record of their convention proceedings. The Library of Congress has microfilmed the convention proceedings of both parties and many libraries have purchased these microfilms. The best reference compendiums are listed below, with the most recently published appearing first.

National Party Conventions, 1831–1992. Washington, DC: Congressional Quarterly, 1995.
 This concise work is the best ready reference guide to conventions. While it does not reprint platforms in their entirety, it does include excerpts and provides a chronology of all the nomination conventions, a list of nominees from all political parties, and a biographical directory of presidential and vice-presidential candidates from 1831 to 1992.

Johnson, Donald B. *National Party Platforms*. 2 vols. 6th rev. ed. Champaign: University of Illinois Press, 1978.

Johnson, Donald B. *National Party Platforms of 1980*. Champaign: University of Illinois Press, 1982.
 These standard reference works are a comprehensive collection of party platforms for all major and minor parties competing at the national level. They contain authenticated copies of platforms for all major and principal minor parties, include the names of all presidential and vice-presidential candidates, and provide the distribution of popular and electoral votes. The material is ar-

ranged in chronological order. Comprehensive indexes to the platforms appear as well.

Chester, Edward W. *A Guide to Political Platforms*. Hamden, CT: Shoe String Press, 1977.
This volume provides a history of the issues relating to each platform. It is an excellent source for secondary information about each platform. The volume covers the early 1830s through 1976.

Newspapers are an invaluable resource for anyone interested in researching national conventions. They are useful not only for their reporting of the proceedings, but also as a record of journalists' perceptions of the convention, issues, and public interest. *The New York Times*, the *Washington Post*, and other major newspapers cover conventions extensively; you should also remember to check the newspapers of the city and state where the conventions were held.

Time, *Newsweek*, and other newsmagazines also provide extensive coverage of national conventions. The *Reader's Guide to Periodical Literature*, the *Public Affairs Information Service Bulletin*, or other indexes should be checked for relevant news stories.

Again, it is useful to check online database services, as they contain the full texts of newspapers, news magazines, television news transcripts, and other news sources. The Internet is another source of information about party positions and conditions.

Campaigns

The following three encyclopedias provide information about presidential campaigns and elections.

Maisel, Sandy L., ed. *Political Parties and Elections in the United States: An Encyclopedia*. New York: Garland Publishing, 1991.
This volume includes fifty essay-length articles and over eleven hundred mini-essays that examine events, concepts, personalities, elections, incumbents, platforms, financing, suffrage, and other topics. The longer essays all include bibliographic references and the work is fully indexed and cross indexed. Much data on individuals, parties, and elections are included.

Running for President: The Candidates and Their Images. 2 vols. New York: Simon and Schuster, 1994.
This two-volume reference work covers the period from 1789 to 1992. Essays offer discussion of a variety of aspects of presiden-

tial campaigns, including style, tactics, and techniques. They also cover the rise of television in campaigns, the role of consultants, and the use of public opinion polls. The work also includes 1,304 illustrations of political paraphernalia, including posters, buttons, bumper stickers, and the like. The essays and illustrations work together to provide a unique visual history of presidential campaigns since 1789.

Shields-West, Eileen. *The World Almanac of Presidential Campaigns.* New York: World Almanac, 1992.
This volume, illustrated by cartoonist Jeff MacNelly, provides information on candidate credentials, conventions, campaign notes, symbols, slogans, songs, paraphernalia, popular labels, and name calling. Information on spending and the vote and a collection of memorable quotes on the subjects are included as well.

Vital Statistics on the Presidency: Washington to Clinton (Washington, DC: Congressional Quarterly, 1995) has an excellent section on campaign finance. The *Congressional Quarterly Weekly Report* and the *National Journal* regularly publish articles based on federal campaign data.

Election Returns

Listed below is the best single source for primary and caucus information.

McGillivray, Alice V. *Presidential Primaries and Caucuses: 1992.* Washington, DC: Congressional Quarterly, 1992.
Designed as a basic reference for the study of the presidential selection process, this new election reference provides official county-by-county results for every presidential primary held in 1992. All returns are gathered from the final, official results from each state authority. This information cannot be found elsewhere in a single volume. A new edition is scheduled to be published every two years.

The following guides are the best sources for presidential election returns. They are listed according to years of coverage, with the most recent appearing first.

Congressional Quarterly. *Guide to U.S. Elections.* 3d ed. Washington, DC: Congressional Quarterly, 1994.
This is the definitive source of statistical data on elections. Included are the complete voting records of elections for the presidency, Congress, and governorships. This volume is an excellent reference guide to all aspects of elections. It offers extensive background material on the history of parties, preference primaries, demographic data, and redistricting. Accompanying each major section of the work is a topical bibliography. The format makes this an especially useful reference work. There are three ways by which to locate information: a detailed table of contents provides an overall view of the scope and coverage of the work; candidate indexes for presidential, gubernatorial, Senate, and House contenders offer a more specific search; and a general index covers all subjects discussed in the work.

Presidential Elections: 1789–1992. Washington, DC: Congressional Quarterly, 1995.
This book traces the presidential electoral process. It includes a series of tables showing votes received by each primary candidate through the 1992 elections, lists covering party nominating conventions and nominated candidates since 1831, a discussion of voting trends and turnout, and tables of state-by-state vote totals and percentages for major candidates. The book uses maps and tables to display electoral college results since 1789. The appendix contains presidential and vice-presidential biographies, texts of constitutional provisions and statutes relating to presidential elections, and a bibliography.

NES CD-ROM.
This CD-ROM, produced in 1995 by the Inter-University Consortium for Political and Social Research in tandem with the National Election Studies, can be used to find election data information. It includes the twenty-two time-series National Election Studies conducted in 1948, 1952, 1956, and biennially from 1958 to 1994. The Cumulative Data File (1952–1992), which merges into a single file those variables included three or more times in the biennial time-series studies, is also included. The NES CD-ROM is available for purchase from the Consortium at the University of Michigan and is available for use at member institutions.

The Election Data Book: A Statistical Portrait of Voting in America. Lanham, MD: Bernan Press, 1993—.

This biennial series presents historical and current statistics on voting results for congressional, senatorial, presidential, and gubernatorial elections. The volume includes more than 150 maps and charts and presents data broken down by state, county, and congressional district on population, race, voting age, registration, turnout, and primary results.

Scammon, Richard M., and Alice V. McGillivray, comps. *America Votes: A Handbook of Contemporary American Election Statistics*. Washington, DC: Congressional Quarterly, 1955—.
This biennial work includes presidential, congressional, and gubernatorial returns, as well as data on primary elections. The total vote (Republican and Democratic), pluralities, and percentages per county and congressional district are reported. Sections on each of the states include a map of the state depicting counties and congressional districts; a geographical breakdown by county for presidential, senatorial, and gubernatorial returns; and tables of congressional returns by district. The volume compiles data since 1928.

McGillivray, Alice V., and Richard M. Scammon. *America at the Polls: A Handbook of Presidential Election Statistics 1920–1992*. Washington, DC: Congressional Quarterly, 1994.
This two-volume set covers presidential election results from Harding through Clinton. Included are state results down to the county level; a summary of popular and electoral college votes; tables of the national presidential vote on a state-by-state basis with both pluralities and percentages noted; census population data by county for each decade; presidential preference primary votes by state and candidate; and full page maps outlining each county. Congressional Quarterly publishes these volumes on two disk sets. The disks contain election results as they appear in the printed volumes in ASCII format suitable to be read into spreadsheet, word processing, or other computer programs.

Thomas, G. Scott. *The Pursuit of the White House: A Handbook of Presidential Election Statistics and History*. New York: Greenwood Press, 1987.
This volume provides a complete statistical and descriptive guide to the presidential elections between 1789 and 1984, including tables that contain data for all major party primaries, conventions, and elections. The book provides profiles of the candidates, parties, and states that shaped the outcome of each election.

Peterson, Svend. *A Statistical History of the American Presidential Elections.* New York: Ungar, 1963.
This volume contains complete statistics for all presidential elections up to 1960. It includes 133 statistical compilations, with tables indicating votes and percentages. The tables are organized according to election, states, and the eleven historical parties examined. It also provides an analysis of each election where a switch of less than one percent of the major party vote would have changed the outcome. Numerous miscellaneous tables of specific interest appear as well. The work is especially useful for information concerning minor parties and candidates.

The following four listings will be of particular interest to the researcher in need of election returns by county. These volumes provide the only sources for county breakdowns of election results between 1836 and 1944.

Robinson, Edgar Eugene. *The Presidential Vote, 1896–1932.* Stanford, CA: Stanford University Press, 1934.

Robinson, Edgar Eugene. *The Presidential Vote 1936: Supplementing the Presidential Vote, 1896–1932.* Stanford, CA: Stanford University Press, 1940.

Robinson, Edgar Eugene. *They Voted for Roosevelt: The Presidential Vote, 1932–1944.* Stanford, CA: Stanford University Press, 1947.
This series provides election returns by state and county for the thirteen presidential elections between 1896 and 1944. These volumes are arranged to facilitate study of all counties for any particular election or a particular county for all elections. Tables indicate the distribution of the presidential vote by section of the country, state, and county and the distribution of party control by the same. Maps and other specific tables are used to illustrate additional dimensions of the election results. The narrative essays provide a good analysis and interpretation of the data.

Burnham, Walter Dean. *Presidential Ballots, 1836–1892.* Baltimore: Johns Hopkins University Press, 1955.
This work is a compilation of voting returns by state and county for presidential elections between 1836 and 1892. It is a backward extension of the series compiled by Edgar E. Robinson (see above). The structure parallels the Robinson series.

The *National Journal* and the *Congressional Quarterly Weekly Report* publish the results of elections in special issues appearing a week or two following the election. For a week-by-week analysis of a campaign and election, these two journals are indispensable, as are *The New York Times* and the *Washington Post*. Online database services can be used for finding primary and election data information on campaign funding and analysis and tracking of campaigns. Transcripts of television and radio broadcasts and the full texts of newspapers appear in the online database services the next day.

Television Coverage

Television news coverage is available to the public through television news archives at various locations in the United States. Because newscasts devote a major portion of each program to governmental issues, they can be of considerable value to the presidential scholar.

Vanderbilt University. Television News Archives. Nashville, TN.
The Television News Archives at Vanderbilt University is the most complete television news archive in the United States. Its holdings include a collection of evening newscasts and special news programs from the major networks since August 1968. The tapes of the news programs are available for a fee.

The Cable Satellite Public Affairs Network (C-SPAN), available on cable TV, is a valuable asset to students of American politics. Started in 1979, this live broadcast of congressional proceedings provides gavel-to-gavel coverage of the House and Senate plus other public affairs programming such as National Press Club speeches, policy addresses, debates, and public policy forums and call-in programs. While C-SPAN focuses on the Congress there is nonetheless a considerable amount of programming related to the presidency, including coverage of presidential candidates and campaigns and presidential policy initiatives under discussion in Congress. C-SPAN broadcasts on two, 24-hour channels; C-SPAN I carries the House and C-SPAN II carries the Senate. There is also a C-SPAN homepage on the World Wide Web and a Gopher on the Internet, whose menu includes information about programs and other activities. The C-SPAN gopher address is *gopher://C-span.org* and the World Wide Web address is *http://www. C-span.org*.

The Public Affairs Video Archives, located at Purdue University, records, catalogs, indexes, and distributes all programming on both channels of C-SPAN. The Archives has recorded and cataloged all C-SPAN programming since October 1987. It has published a CD-ROM product entitled Public Affairs Chronicle, first issued for 1991. This CD-ROM product is a database of over 12,500 primary source public affairs events, including events covered on C-SPAN as well as those that are not. The database contains over 8,700 full text transcripts that can be searched and read. A CD-ROM for 1992 is in progress and plans are under way for more recent years. This product is the best way to search all events covered by C-SPAN. For more information about these services and programs you should contact the Archives directly.

Transcripts of television news programs can also be found on the on-line database series—in particular, check LEXIS/NEXIS. Again, Broadcast News on CD-ROM (see page 20) includes the transcripts of television broadcasts as well as many other sources of news and analysis.

Oral Histories

Oral histories are another important resource for research on the presidency. They are excellent primary source material. The following three oral history collections, published by University Publications of America, focus on the presidency:

The Harry S Truman Oral Histories Collection.

The John F. Kennedy Presidential Oral History Collection.

Oral Histories of the Johnson Administration.

Interest Groups

In this section we list some directories that identify and provide information on lobbyists and other associations and organizations involved in the political process. While these directories provide a considerable amount of information about interest groups, some of the sources cited earlier are also useful. Both the *Congressional Quarterly Weekly Report* and the *National Journal* offer extensive coverage of interest groups. Newspaper and magazine literature supply important information, too, for their coverage goes behind the scenes to detail the efforts of various political groups. Trade, industrial, and professional journals have regular columns or sections on national politics. The *Business Periodicals Index*, the *Applied Science and Technology Index*, and the *Public Affairs Information Service Bulletin* can all be used to direct research to trade magazines. Finally, the online database services provide a wealth of information on interest groups and lobbyists.

American Lobbyists Directory. Detroit: Gale, 1990—.
This volume contains information on registered lobbyists at the

federal and state levels. It includes separate federal and state lob-
byist listings. An organization index that lists organizations repre-
sented by lobbyists and a subject index that lists lobbies according
to subject area are provided.

Directory of Washington Representatives of American Associations and Industry.
Washington, DC: Columbia Books, 1977—.
This directory includes lobbyists, legal advisors, information col-
lectors and consultants representing public interest groups, cor-
porations, labor unions, trade and professional associations, state
and local governments, political action committees, and foreign
governments. The information is arranged in two alphabetically
cross-referenced lists. The first lists representatives by name, address, and date of registration. The second lists organizations by
the address, name, and title of their representatives and includes
a brief description of their activities. Subject and country indexes
are provided.

*Directory of Washington Lobbyists, Lawyers, and Interest Groups in the Wash-
ington Metropolitan Area.* Washington, DC: Amward Publications,
1993—.
This semiannual directory offers a list of lobbyists active in the
Washington metropolitan area.

Public Interest Profiles. Washington, DC: Congressional Quarterly, 1977—.
This volume provides detailed information on about 250 public
interest and public policy organizations. It notes budget and
funding services for each organization, the board of directors of
the organizations, their publications and methods of operation,
and information on political action committees.

Washington Representatives. Washington, DC: Columbia Books, 1979—.
This annual directory contains a list of representatives, a list of
organizations, a subject index, and a country index. In addition,
it offers a list of the congressional committees, along with their
membership, and regulatory agencies that are the focus of lobbying efforts.

Public Opinion Polls

Polls are conducted on a variety of topics related to the presidency, including foreign affairs and economics. Perhaps the best known are those
measuring the president's "approval rating." There are several ways to

find information about polls that focus on the presidency and presidential elections. Below we have listed the guides to the Gallup Polls. Hundreds of other organizations conduct polls as well. The *American Public Opinion Index*, published by Opinion Research Services, is an annual index to major polls done throughout the United States at the national, state, and local levels. Begun in 1981, this annual volume is an excellent place to look for information on polls. For Gallup Polls consult the sources listed below.

Gallup, George Horace. *The Gallup Poll: Public Opinion, 1935–1971.* 3 vols. New York: Random House, 1972.
This is a complete collection of the Gallup Polls from 1935 to 1971. An index in the third volume provides easy subject access to the polls. Supplementary volumes have been published covering the next six years, then annual volumes starting with 1978.

The Gallup Poll: Public Opinion, 1972–1977. Wilmington, DE: Scholarly Resources, 1978.

The Gallup Poll: Public Opinion, . . . Wilmington, DE: Scholarly Resources, 1979—.

Gallup Opinion Index Report: Political, Social and Economic Trends. Princeton, NJ: Gallup International, 1965—.
The *Report* is published monthly, with special issues appearing from time to time. The surveys are based on a population of at least 1,500 respondents selected according to scientific protocol. The surveys include findings on presidential popularity and performance as well as on a variety of campaign and election issues.

Audiovisual Materials

Video cassettes are another resource available for the study of the presidency. They tend to give the viewer a better understanding of how the presidency works. The four-part series *The Power Game*, written and narrated by journalist and reporter Hedrick Smith, includes one part entitled "The Presidency." It is available from PBS. Video Insights distributes several video cassettes on the presidency, including "Role of the Chief Executive," "The Executive Branch," and "United States Presidents: Personality and Politics." Aristotle Political Campaign Videos has released a series of tapes on presidential primary and election commercials. They include "Best Campaign Commercials of 1992, Presidential Primary"; "Best

Campaign Commercials of 1992, Presidential General"; "Best Campaign Commercials of 1988, Presidential Primary"; "Best Campaign Commercials of 1988, Presidential General"; "Best Campaign Commercials of 1984"; and "Best of Old Campaign Commercials."

Audio cassettes are a further source of information. National Public Radio sells a wide variety of cassettes related to the presidency. Topics include campaigning, elections, and National Press Club speeches. Many libraries collect video and audio cassettes, so be sure to check on what is available.

Internet Sources

The Internet is a worldwide network of computers. Users include individuals, schools, libraries, universities, and businesses as well as many other groups and organizations around the world. Access to software programs, library catalogs, databases, documents, electronic mail, images and sound, and electronic discussion groups make the Internet invaluable. Perhaps the best way to introduce yourself to this resource is to use any of the many books that describe how it works and what it includes. Some of the better known of these are *The Internet Directory*, *The Whole Internet: User's Guide and Catalog*, *The Internet Complete Reference*, and the *World Wide Web Unleashed*. The Internet is growing and changing daily. System addresses, source directories, and file names change. Sometimes a remote system is unavailable and some things even disappear, so users need to have patience.

All kinds of federal government information is available to Internet users, including White House briefings, Supreme Court decisions, and census data. Material related directly to the presidency includes executive branch directories; the full text of the budget; the full texts of platforms; the full texts of presidential publications appearing in the *Federal Register*, such as proclamations and executive orders; and White House information, such as major policy statements, daily press briefings, speeches, and the president's daily schedule. This represents just a slice of what is available on the Internet, which grows daily. A good place to start, however, would be the White House home page on the World Wide Web (*http://www.whitehouse.gov/*). Set up and maintained by the White House, it includes the full texts of daily press releases, the week's speeches, and the *U.S. Budget* and the *State of the Union Address* as well as other information about the president, the vice president, the executive branch, the cabinet, and the independent agencies and commissions. Another useful home page on the World Wide Web that provides presidential inaugural addresses and other selected addresses can be found at the following address: *http://grid.let.rug.nl/~welling/usa/presidents/addresses.html*.

Many other sources are described in Blake Gumprecht's second edition of *Internet Sources of Government Information* (Philadelphia: Temple University, 1994). Current and future editions of this work can be retrieved via Gopher and anonymous FTP from the University of Michigan's Clearinghouse of Subject-Oriented Internet Resource Guides (*gopher://una.hh.lib.umich.edu*). Once there go into the "inetdirs" folder, followed by the "guides on the social sciences" folder. The World Wide Web address is *http://www.lib.umich.edu/chouse*. This second edition includes more than 325 sources of information and provides both Gopher sources and Telnet addresses when known, although the preferred source is often a Gopher source because of the ease of the software. The guide is also accessible via e-mail.

Bruce Maxwell's *How to Access the Federal Government on the Internet: Washington Online* (Washington, DC: Congressional Quarterly, 1996) is another good guide to Internet resources. It provides detailed descriptions of more than 250 Internet sites and discusses how to access the texts of bills, lists of holdings at the National Archives, and electronic sources at the Library of Congress. The *Federal Internet Source*, published in 1995 by National Journal, contains up-to-date descriptions, listings, addresses, and home pages of more than 500 federal, state, and other political Internet sites.

One source on the Internet that offers a variety of government information is the Library of Congress's MARVEL, *marvel.loc.gov* on the gopher. You can also get to MARVEL from the Library of Congress's home page *http://www.loc.gov* on the World Wide Web. MARVEL provides the *United States Code* and access to GPO ACCESS. The GPO ACCESS database includes the *Congressional Record* (starting with 1994), the *History of Bills* (starting with 1994), the *United States Code* (starting with 1994), *Congressional Bills* (starting with the 103d Congress), and the *Federal Register* (starting with 1994) and numerous other databases.

The Library of Congress has initiated a new electronic tool. Dubbed THOMAS, it provides access to government information over the World Wide Web on the Internet. THOMAS gathers several government resources into one place, including the full text of legislation, the full text of the *Congressional Record*, and the C-SPAN Gopher. It supplements much of the same online information found in the MARVEL system, but THOMAS offers hypertext links. THOMAS is accessible on the World Wide Web at the following address: *http://thomas.loc.gov*. Another World Wide Web site is PoliticsUSA (*http://PoliticsUSA.com*). Created by National Journal and the American Political Network, it includes up-to-the-minute news from the White House, Congress, and campaign organizations.

There are several gophers of interest to researchers of the presidency. For example, a C-SPAN Gopher includes information about programs, press releases, voting data, and how to send e-mail to C-SPAN. The C-SPAN Gopher address is *gopher://C-span.org/*. C-SPAN also has its own home page on the World Wide Web. Web browsers will find the C-SPAN home page at *http://www.C-span.org*. Congressional Quarterly has the CQ Gopher. Through it you will find lead stories of the current *Congressional Quarterly Weekly Report*, articles from the Special Reports, weekly news briefs from *CQ Researcher*, the status of appropriations bills and other major legislation from CQ's WASHINGTON ALERT, results of key roll call votes, information on presidential elections, and much more. The CQ Gopher is offered free of charge to Internet users. To access, Internet users with gopher client/service should point their gopher at *gopher://gopher.cqalert.com/*.

Another useful book by Bruce Maxwell is *How to Access the Government's Electronic Bulletin Boards 1996: Washington Online* (Washington, DC: Congressional Quarterly, 1995). It provides easy-to-understand explanations of how to log on to federal bulletin boards and then how to use them. It also gives detailed descriptions of what each board offers. A sampling of some of the information available through free federal bulletin boards includes lists of contacts at federal agencies; government statistics on income, poverty, population growth, immigration, taxes, government revenue, and school financing; and transcripts of presidential speeches. Most of the bulletin boards have menu systems. The book shows how to navigate the menu and how to download the bulletin board information. Written in nontechnical language, it is filled with numerous practical tips and provides the most comprehensive, up-to-date listing of free federal government bulletin boards available.

Archives

Archives contain original documents, such as letters, memos, reports, and other forms of primary research material. Collections of presidential papers and correspondence can be found in the Library of Congress, presidential libraries, and other special libraries. The following guides are useful in locating relevant archival material.

Schnick, Frank L., Renee Schnick, and Mark Carroll. *Records of the Presidency: Presidential Papers and Libraries from Washington to Reagan.* Phoenix, AZ: Oryx Press, 1989.

Hyland, Pat. *Presidential Libraries and Museums: An Illustrated Guide.* Washington, DC: Congressional Quarterly, 1995.

The Library of Congress is the major archival center for presidential papers. There are twenty-three groups of presidential papers, ranging from the papers of George Washington to those of Calvin Coolidge. The Manuscript Division of the Library of Congress organized and indexed over two million manuscripts for the Presidential Papers Program. They have microfilmed the presidential papers and made them available to many research libraries. Reproductions of its holdings are generally available to other libraries as well.

The National Archives and Records Services administers ten presidential libraries throughout the country. These libraries contain the papers and files of the presidents as well as correspondence of the presidents and their associates. The libraries' holdings vary, but presidential papers and White House files are found in each. The individual libraries provide guides to their holdings. The researcher must apply to the presidential library of interest, stating his or her research topic. Presidential libraries have been established for the following ten presidents: Herbert Hoover, Franklin D. Roosevelt, Harry S. Truman, Dwight D. Eisenhower, John F. Kennedy, Lyndon B. Johnson, Richard M. Nixon, Gerald R. Ford, Jimmy Carter, and Ronald Reagan.

Additional libraries hold collections of presidential materials. These include the Buffalo and Erie County Historical Society, which holds a major collection of Millard Fillmore's papers; the Hoover Institution on War, Revolution and Peace, which houses manuscripts of Herbert Hoover; the Massachusetts Historical Society, where the papers of John Adams and John Quincy Adams are found; the Manuscript Department of the Historical Society of Pennsylvania, which holds the James Buchanan papers; the Ohio Historical Society, which holds the papers of Warren G. Harding; and the Rutherford B. Hayes Presidential Center, which contains the papers of Hayes.

In 1980, University Publications of America began publishing a Presidential Documents series. Issued on microfilm with accompanying printed guides, the sets include minutes of cabinet meetings, daily diaries, and assorted collections containing a variety of presidential papers. Listed below are some of the sets that have been published to date:

The Presidential Diaries of Henry Morganthau, Jr. (1938–1945)

Map Room Messages of President Roosevelt (1942–1945)

Map Room Messages of President Truman (1945–1946)

Potsdam Conference Documents

Minutes and Documents of the Cabinet Meetings of President Eisenhower (1953–1961)

Appointment Book of President Kennedy (1961–1963)

President Kennedy and the Press

Daily Diary of President Johnson (1963–1969)

Minutes and Documents of the Cabinet Meetings of President Johnson (1963–1969)

Franklin D. Roosevelt and Foreign Affairs: Second Series, 1937–1939

Franklin D. Roosevelt: Diary and Itineraries/Usher Books

New Deal Economic Policies: FDR and the Congress, 1933–1938

President Franklin D. Roosevelt's Office Files, 1933–1945

President Harry S Truman's Office Files, 1945–1953

The Diaries of Dwight D. Eisenhower, 1953–1961

Papers of the President's Science Advisory Committee, 1957–1961

President Dwight D. Eisenhower's Office Files, 1953–1961

President Eisenhower's Meetings with Legislative Leaders, 1953–1961

The John F. Kennedy 1960 Campaign

President John F. Kennedy's Office Files, 1961–1963

Political Activities of the Johnson White House, 1963–1969

Papers of the Nixon White House

Congressional Quarterly has published two volumes that contain a variety of historical documents on the presidency.

Nelson, Michael, ed. *Historic Documents on the Presidency: 1776–1989.* Washington, DC: Congressional Quarterly, 1989.
This volume contains eighty historically significant documents. Spanning over two hundred years, this resource makes it possible to examine material from many presidencies in a single volume. Documents range from presidential speeches, statements, and proclamations to the *Federalist Papers* and Supreme Court decisions. Each document is accompanied by an introduction that sets the context.

Nelson, Michael, ed. *Historic Documents on Presidential Elections 1787–1988.* Washington, DC: Congressional Quarterly, 1991.
This volume includes seventy key speeches and documents in one convenient reference. Materials range from the Constitutional

Convention debates on presidential selection in 1787 to the Bush-Dukakis debates of 1988.

Data Archives

The major social science data archive is the Inter-University Consortium for Political and Social Research at the University of Michigan. For more information about its holdings, you should consult the Consortium's most recent *Guide to Resources and Services*. The *Guide* includes information on training programs, classes, remote access computer assistance, and how to obtain data and codebooks. The listing of archival holdings provides the name of the data collector, the title and detailed description of the data file, and related publications that have used the data. Numerous data files relate to the president. For example there are files containing election returns, public opinion polls, and many other subjects related to the presidency. In 1995 the Consortium in tandem with the National Election Studies issued the NES CD-ROM. This product contains the twenty-two time-series National Election Studies conducted in 1948, 1952, and 1956 and biennially from 1958 to 1994. The Cumulative Data File (1952–1992), which merges into a single file those variables included three or more times in the biennial time-series studies is also included. The NES CD-ROM is available for purchase from the Consortium, and is available for use at member institutions.

Administrative Law

The *Federal Register* and the *Code of Federal Regulations* contain current compilations of all rules and regulations issued by executive departments and agencies. The former is an invaluable tool for monitoring rules and regulations, as it is the only publication that prints all rules adopted by agencies. Issued daily, the *Federal Register* contains presidential documents, rules and regulations, proposed rules and notices to the public of proposed rules, notices and miscellaneous documents that are of interest to the public, and notices of meetings. The *Federal Register* is basically a daily update of the *Code of Federal Regulations*. When an agency adopts a new rule, it is first published in the *Federal Register*. When the *Code of Federal Regulations* is updated, these newly adopted rules are inserted into their proper places in the *Code of Federal Regulations*.

The *Federal Register* provides a number of bibliographic tools. These "finding aids" are printed at the end of each issue. The Contents section contains a complete listing of all proposed and final rules, as well as notices, arranged by agency. Each entry includes the beginning page number of the document and a brief description. The Notices section is arranged by agency name and provides the date when scheduled meetings are to be held. The *Code of Federal Regulations* Parts Affected in This Issue section is a listing of titles and parts of the *Code of Federal Regulations* that have been or will be affected by rules contained within that day's issue. There is also a cumulative list noting titles and parts affected for the month. The Reader Aids section is intended to assist the user in finding specific information in the *Federal Register*. The Information and Assistance section offers a listing of Office of Federal Register telephone numbers to call for specific questions. Finally, the *Federal Register* Pages and Dates section provides a table listing inclusive page numbers and the dates that correspond to them for the current month's *Federal Register*.

One important finding aid for the *Federal Register* is published separately. The *Federal Register Index* appears monthly and annually. It is arranged by agency and provides citations to all proposed and final rules and notices that have been printed in the *Federal Register* over the preceding quarter or year.

The *Code of Federal Regulations* is a codification of the rules published in the *Federal Register*. Revised annually, the *Code* is arranged into fifty titles, each representing a broad subject area. Each title contains regulations pertaining to a single subject area and consists of one or more chapters. Each chapter presents a single agency's regulations. The chapters are further divided into parts, then parts into sections. If necessary, sections are broken down into paragraphs. Because most titles cover a broad area, specific regulations will generally be contained in more than one book, though all of a particular agency's regulations will normally appear in a single title.

One-quarter of the *Code* is revised and reissued every three months. Consequently, at the end of each year the complete *Code of Federal Regulations* has been revised. The revision date appears on the cover of each volume.

Every volume of the *Code* includes a Table of *CFR* Titles and Chapters, which lists the subject areas of the regulations contained in each title and the name of the agency for the corresponding chapter. Finding aids follow the codified material. Every volume of the *Code* includes an alphabetical list of agencies whose regulations are codified and a citation to the title and chapter where the agency's regulations are located. There is also a List of CFR Sections affected. All changes in that volume of the *Code* published previously in the *Federal Register* are enumerated in this list.

The *CFR Index* appears separately from the *Code*. Revised semiannually, this volume consists of an index arranged by agency name and subject heading and covers rules currently codified in the *Code*. Citations refer to the title and parts of the *Code* where the rules pertaining to a subject or agency can be found. Also included in the *CFR Index* are agency-prepared indexes for each volume of the *Code*; a parallel table of statutory authorities and rules; a list of *CFR* titles, chapters, subchapters, and parts; and an alphabetical list of agencies appearing in the *Code*.

Finally, the *List of CFR Sections Affected (LSA)* is a cumulative update to the *Code* that is published monthly. The starting date for each title in the *LSA* is the date when the volume of the *Code* containing that title was last revised. The *LSA* is intended to assist users of the *Code* in finding amendments published in the *Federal Register*. The entries are arranged by *Code* title, chapter, part, and section, and they denote the change made. The *LSA* also contains a checklist of current *CFR* volumes for the present month, a parallel table of authorities and rules, and a table of *Federal Register* issue pages and dates. The *LSA* allows the researcher to find out what new rules, amendments, or proposed rules have been promulgated since the *Code* was last updated without having to go through numerous issues of the *Federal Register*.

Finding Tools

While the *Federal Register* and the *Code of Federal Regulations* are the primary sources of rules and regulations, there are other indexes for finding administrative citations available. One is the *CIS Federal Register Index*, discussed on pages 29, 30, and 32. The full text of the *Federal Register* is also available on the Internet through GPO ACCESS, starting with 1994. The CD/FR: Compact Disk Federal Register is a CD-ROM index to the *Federal Register*, published in 1993. This product, plus the one listed below, is easier to use than the indexes and finding aids found in the *Federal Register* and the *United States Code*. The *Index to the Code of Federal Regulations* (Bethesda, MD: Congressional Information Service, 1977—) is an annual service with a detailed subject index that allows a search of all fifty titles at once. You can search a general or specific subject and be referred to all the relevant parts and subparts. There are two geographical indexes as well. The first indexes regulations regarding political jurisdictions such as states, countries, and cities. The second cites properties administered by the federal government, such as parks and military bases. Two additional indexes can save you time if you already have a citation. A list of descriptive headings gives headings assigned to each part of the *Code*, and a list of reserved headings indicates which parts of the *CFR* have been designated reserved, either for future use or because they have been vacated from use. Starting in 1991 there are also quarterly updates and an index by *CFR* section number. Be sure to check which CD-ROM products and other commercial indexes are available in the libraries you use.

Statutory Law

Briefly, legislation is passed into law in the following way. A member of one of the chambers of Congress introduces a bill. This bill is referred to a committee and then to a subcommittee, which may hold hearings on it and amend it. The committee then issues its report. The bill comes before the full chamber for floor action where it may be debated and amended. If it passes, the bill is sent to the other chamber, where it goes through the same process. Often, each chamber is simultaneously working on the same or a similar bill. When both chambers have passed their versions of a bill, they reconcile any differences by agreeing to or modifying the amendments of the other chamber or by sending the bill to a conference committee. The conference committee hammers out a bill acceptable to both bodies. Once both the Senate and the House have agreed on the specific language, the bill is sent to the White House for presidential approval and signature into law. If the president vetoes the bill, the Congress has the option of trying to override his veto.

Finding Tools

There are numerous finding tools, some published by the federal government and others produced by commercial companies, that are used to trace the course of a bill through Congress as well as identify what publications exist. Here we will describe a few of these sources. We offer brief annotations to what are generally very complex publications. However, the intent of this section is not to provide elaborate instructions for their use, but only to acquaint the researcher with them. In addition to the sources listed here, many of the finding tools to presidential documents we have already discussed are also useful for legislative research. We should stress once again that the best way to gain full knowledge and command of these finding tools is through repeated use.

Calendars of the United States House of Representatives and History of Legislation. Washington, DC: U.S. Government Printing Office, 1951—.
The *Calendars* is published daily when the House is in session, and each issue is cumulative, which makes it a useful guide to legislative action. Each Monday there is a subject index to all legislation action to date in both the House and Senate. House and Senate bills passed or pending are arranged numerically in a table. There is also information concerning committee schedules and the weekly House floor schedule on the House Gopher.

Congress in Print. Washington, DC: Congressional Quarterly, 1977—.
This publication, issued forty-eight times a year, lists all committee hearings, prints, reports, calendars, public laws, and other congressional documents released the previous week. Online access is provided through CQ's WASHINGTON ALERT.

Congressional Index. Washington, DC: Commerce Clearing House, 1937/38—.
This weekly publication indexes congressional bills and resolutions and lists their current status. The index is designed to enable the user to follow the progress of legislation. It contains a section on voting records in which all roll call votes are reported. Vetoes and subsequent congressional actions are recorded as well.

Congressional Monitor. Washington, DC: Congressional Quarterly, 1965—.
The *Monitor* lists all hearings to be held on the date of issue as well as those that have been scheduled for the future. Selected congressional press conferences, speeches, and interest group meetings are listed as well. Floor action taken the previous week or scheduled for the current week is also listed. The *Monitor* includes a two-page summary of legislative action from the previous day and highlights of events scheduled to take place on the day of issue. It includes committee votes, staff changes, and behind-the-scenes news. Online access is available through CQ's WASHINGTON ALERT.

Congressional Record Scanner. Washington, DC: Congressional Quarterly.
The *Scanner* is an abstract of the day's *Congressional Record*. It offers a sentence summary of every speech, bill, report, and action on the floor. It is published one day after the printing of the *Record* itself. Speeches are listed by name of members and the corresponding page number of the *Record*.

Congressional Roll Call. Washington, DC: Congressional Quarterly, 1970—.
This annual series began with the first session of the 91st Congress. Each volume opens with an analysis and legislative description of key votes on major issues. This is followed by special voting studies, such as freshman voting, bipartisanship, voting participation, and so forth. The remainder of the volume is a member-by-member analysis chronologically arranged of all roll call votes in the House and Senate. There is also a roll call subject

index. In the compilation of roll call votes, a brief synopsis of each bill, the total vote, and vote by party affiliation appears.

United States Code. Washington, DC: U.S. Government Printing Office, 1926—.
The *Code* is a compilation of all federal laws in force. The laws are arranged by subject under fifty titles. An index volume contains a table of all title and chapter headings and a subject index to all sections. The Superintendent of Documents has issued the U.S. Code on CD-ROM. It includes the current *United States Code* in force on January 2, 1992. This full text CD-ROM provides access to all fifty titles. You can do a broad subject search or a specific search for known items. The *United States Code*, starting with the laws of permanent and general effect as of January 1994, is also available on the Internet through GPO ACCESS.

United States Code Annotated. St. Paul, MN: West Publishing Co., 1927–.
This annual set reprints the *United States Code* and provides extensive annotations, legal notes, analytic comments, and legislative histories. This supplemental material is invaluable for anyone interested in researching the original intent and later interpretation of a statute.

Legislative Histories

The key to legislative tracing is obtaining a bill or statute number. It is then relatively easy to compile a legislative history and identify all relevant documents. Finding the bill or statute number is not difficult. Because most finding tools to legislative action are indexed in a variety of ways (for example, by name of individual, committee, report number, subject), just a single piece of information about a bill or law can be used to identify its number. Knowing who introduced a bill or to which committee it was referred can lead to the bill or statute number through use of a name or committee index. If no specific information is known, it is necessary to use a subject approach. The subject indexing in these guides is generally very good. Even if you have only a general knowledge of the substance of a bill or statute, a subject index will lead to its number.

A legislative history would include the following:

1. A history of related legislative activities and publications both prior and subsequent to the bill in question.

2. Materials and recommendations made by executive departments concerning the bill.

3. Materials and recommendations made by special interest groups participating in the legislative process.

4. Statements made by sponsors when introducing a bill or statements made by members that are not part of the debate itself.

5. Statements of the president, either messages or comments, on signing the bill.

6. Any relevant court cases and decisions that relate to the interpretation of the law.

7. Useful secondary analysis and histories, including journal and newspaper articles identified by using indexes, CD-ROMs, or online databases, as well as material from:

   Congressional Quarterly Weekly Report
   National Journal
   Washington Post
   The New York Times

8. A search on online information services for background information as well as information and documents about the legislation itself. This would include searches on:

   CQ's WASHINGTON ALERT
   LEGI-SLATE
   LEXIS/NEXIS
   WESTLAW

9. A search on the Internet for background information as well as information and documents about the legislation itself.

10. A chronological account of how a bill has passed, or is passing, through Congress, including dates, committees, actions taken, and votes, and an examination of documents relating to the passage of a bill.

For a more detailed outline of which finding tools to use at each step of the legislative process, consult Martin and Goehlert's *How to Research Congress* (Washington, DC: Congressional Quarterly, 1996).

Case Law

Supreme Court decisions are first issued as "slip opinions." These are published within three days and are available in depository libraries. The decisions of the Supreme Court are published in the five current reports listed below. A useful introductory guide to the judicial process and how opinions are written can be found in T. R. van Geel's *Understanding Supreme Court Opinions* (New York: Longman, 1991).

U.S. Supreme Court. *United States Reports*. Washington, DC: U.S. Government Printing Office, 1790—.
This annual publication contains the official text of all opinions of the Supreme Court. Also included are tables of cases reported, cases and statutes cited, miscellaneous materials, and a subject index. All written reports and most *per curiam* reports of decisions are printed. Beginning with the 1970 term, chamber opinions are included.

U.S. Law Week. Washington, DC: Bureau of National Affairs, 1933—.
This weekly periodical includes important sections on the Supreme Court. It contains four appendices: a topical index, a table of cases, a docket number table, and a proceedings section. In addition to containing the full texts of all decisions, this resource includes information on new statutes and agency rulings. This tool's most valuable feature is its quick publication of Court decisions.

U.S. Supreme Court. *Supreme Court Reporter*. St. Paul, MN: West Publishing Co., 1983—.
This weekly, private publication contains annotated reports and indexes of case names. It also includes opinions of the justices in chambers.

U.S. Supreme Court. *United States Supreme Court Reports: Lawyers' Edition*. Rochester, NY: Lawyers Co-Operative Publishing Co., 1970—.
This annual service includes all Supreme Court cases. It also contains numerous *per curiam* decisions not found elsewhere and offers individual summaries of the majority and dissenting opinions and counsel briefs. The index to annotations can be used to find the legal notes for each case.

United States Supreme Court Bulletin. Washington, DC: Commerce Clearing House, 1936—.
This is a looseleaf service that contains current Supreme Court decisions and a docket of Court cases. This resource is especially useful for research on the current Court.

Digests of Supreme Court Decisions

There are two excellent finding tools that identify digests of Supreme Court decisions by subject and case name.

Digest of United States Supreme Court Reports, Annotated with Case Annotations, Dissenting and Separate Decisions since 1900. Rochester, NY: Lawyers Co-Operative Publishing Co., 1948—.

United States Supreme Court Digest. St. Paul, MN: West Publishing Co., 1940—.

Briefs and Records of the Supreme Court

Briefs and records are valuable resources for understanding the ultimate outcome of a case as well as the interpretation of a statute or administrative rule. While most libraries do not receive the briefs and records that are submitted to the Supreme Court, many do have them available on microfiche. The Congressional Information Service publishes the following two series on microfiche: the *U.S. Supreme Court Records and Briefs* and *Oral Arguments of the U.S. Supreme Court.* LEXIS/NEXIS also contains briefs beginning in 1979. Other sources for briefs and arguments include those listed below.

Kurland, Philip B., and Gerhard Casper. *Landmark Briefs and Arguments of the Supreme Court of the United States: Constitutional Law.* Frederick, MD: University Publications of America, 1975 .
This series covers hundreds of constitutional cases since 1793. The series includes facsimile reproductions of briefs as they were originally filed at the Supreme Court and transcripts of oral arguments as provided by the Supreme Court Library. Beginning with the volumes for the 1989–1990 term, the series contains the texts of all Court decisions.

U.S. National Archives and Records Service. *Tape Recordings of Oral Arguments before the U.S. Supreme Court.* Washington, DC: National Archives and Records Service, 1955—.
These tapes of oral arguments are available for purchase only after three years have elapsed.

U.S. Supreme Court. *Records and Briefs.* Washington, DC: U.S. Government Printing Office, 1832—.
Relatively few libraries receive copies of the briefs and records submitted to the Supreme Court.

Selected Bibliography on the Presidency and Presidents

Perspectives on the Presidency

Bailey, Harry A., Jr., and Jay M. Shaftitz, eds. *The American Presidency: Historical and Contemporary Perspectives*. Chicago: Dorsey Press, 1988.

Beard, Charles A. *The Presidents in American History: Brought Forward since 1948*. Rev. ed. New York: Messner, 1973.

Binkley, Wilfred E. *The Man in the White House: His Powers and Duties*. Rev. ed. Baltimore: Johns Hopkins University Press, 1964.

Corwin, Edward S., and Louis W. Koenig. *The Presidency Today*. New York: New York University Press, 1956.

Cronin, Thomas E. *Rethinking the Presidency*. Boston: Little, Brown, 1982.

———. *The State of the Presidency*. 2d ed. Boston: Little, Brown, 1980.

———, ed. *Inventing the American Presidency*. Lawrence: University Press of Kansas, 1989.

Cronin, Thomas E., and Rexford G. Tugwell. *The Presidency Reappraised*. 2d ed. New York: Praeger, 1977.

Cunliffe, Marcus. *The Presidency*. 3d ed. Boston: Houghton Mifflin, 1987.

Davis, Vincent, ed. *The Post-Imperial Presidency*. New York: Praeger, 1980.

Diclerico, Robert E. *The American President.* 4th ed. Englewood Cliffs, NJ: Prentice-Hall, 1995.

Edwards, George C., III., and Stephen J. Wayne. *Studying the Presidency.* Knoxville: University of Tennessee Press, 1983.

Edwards, George C., III, John H. Kessel, and Bert A. Rockman, eds. *Researching the Presidency: Vital Questions, New Approaches.* Pittsburgh: University of Pittsburgh Press, 1993.

Ferrell, Robert H. *Ill-Advised: Presidential Health and Public Trust.* Columbia: University of Missouri Press, 1992.

Greenstein, Fred I., ed. *Leadership in the Modern Presidency.* Cambridge, MA: Harvard University Press, 1988.

Hargrove, Erwin C., and Michael Nelson. *Presidents, Politics, and Policy.* Baltimore: Johns Hopkins University Press, 1984.

Heclo, Hugh, and Lester M. Salamon, eds. *The Illusion of Presidential Government.* Boulder, CO: Westview Press, 1981.

Hinckley, Barbara. *The Symbolic Presidency: How Presidents Portray Themselves.* New York: Routledge, 1990.

Jones, Charles O. *The Presidency in a Separated System.* Washington: Brookings Institution, 1994.

Koenig, Louis W. *The Chief Executive.* 5th ed. New York: Harcourt Brace Jovanovich, 1986.

Laski, Harold J. *The American Presidency: An Interpretation.* New York: Grosset and Dunlop, 1940.

Leuchtenburg, William E. *In the Shadow of FDR: From Harry Truman to Ronald Reagan.* Rev. ed. Ithaca, NY: Cornell University Press, 1989.

McConnell, Grant. *The Modern Presidency.* 2d ed. New York: St. Martin's Press, 1976.

McDonald, Forrest. *The American Presidency: An Intellectual History.* Lawrence: University Press of Kansas, 1994.

Milkis, Sidney M., and Michael Nelson. *The American Presidency: Origins and Development, 1776–1993.* 2d ed. Washington, DC: CQ Press, 1994.

Milkis, Sidney M., and Nelson, Michael. *The Presidency and the Political System.* 4th ed. Washington, DC: CQ Press, 1994.

Nichols, David K. *The Myth of the Modern Presidency.* University Park: Pennsylvania State University, 1994.

Page, Benjamin I., and Mark P. Petracca. *The American Presidency.* New York: McGraw-Hill, 1983.

Pfiffner, James P. *The Modern Presidency.* New York: St. Martin's Press, 1994.

Pious, Richard M. *The American Presidency.* New York: Basic Books, 1979.

Polsby, Nelson W., ed. *The Modern Presidency.* New York: Random House, 1973.

Reedy, George E. *The Presidency.* New York: Arno, 1975.

———. *The Presidency in Flux.* New York: Columbia University Press, 1973.

———. *The Twilight of the Presidency: From Johnson to Reagan.* New York: World Publishing, 1987.

Rossiter, Clinton L. *The American Presidency.* 3d ed. New York: Harcourt Brace Jovanovich, 1987.

Schlesinger, Arthur M., Jr. *The Imperial Presidency.* Boston: Houghton Mifflin, 1989.

Seligman, Lester G., and Cary R. Covington. *The Coalitional Presidency.* Chicago: Dorsey Press, 1989.

Stanwood, Edward. *A History of the Presidency.* 3d ed. 2 vols. Boston: Houghton Mifflin, 1928.

Thomas, Norman C., and Joseph A. Pika. *The Politics of the Presidency.* 4th ed. Washington, DC: CQ Press, 1996.

Thompson, Kenneth W. *The President and the Public Philosophy.* Baton Rouge: Louisiana State University Press, 1981.

Tugwell, Rexford G. *How They Became President: Thirty-Five Ways to the White House.* New York: Simon and Schuster, 1968.

Wildavsky, Aaron B. *The Beleaguered Presidency.* New Brunswick, NJ: Transaction Publishers, 1991.

———. *The Presidency.* Boston: Little, Brown, 1969.

———, ed. *Perspectives on the Presidency.* Boston: Little, Brown, 1975.

The Presidency and the Constitution

Barber, Sotirios A. *The Constitution and the Delegation of Congressional Power.* Chicago: University of Chicago Press, 1975.

Berger, Raoul. *Impeachment: The Constitutional Problems.* Cambridge, MA: Harvard University Press, 1973.

Black, Charles L. *Impeachment: A Handbook.* New Haven, CT: Yale University Press, 1974.

Bowen, Catherine D. *Miracle at Philadelphia: The Story of the Constitutional Convention, May to September 1787.* Boston: Little, Brown, 1986.

Burgess, Susan R. *Contest for Constitutional Authority: The Abortion and War Powers Debates.* Lawrence: University Press of Kansas, 1992.

Fisher, Louis. *The Constitution between Friends: Congress, the President, and the Law.* New York: St. Martin's Press, 1978.

———. *Constitutional Conflicts between Congress and the President.* 3d ed. Princeton, NJ: Princeton University Press, 1991.

Sundquist, James L. *Constitutional Reform and Effective Government.* Rev. ed. Washington, DC: Brookings Institution, 1992.

Thach, Charles C., Jr. *The Creation of the Presidency 1775–1789: A Study in Constitutional History.* Baltimore: Johns Hopkins University Press, 1923.

Presidential Powers

Berger, Raoul. *Executive Privilege: A Constitutional Myth.* Cambridge, MA: Harvard University Press, 1974.

Binkley, Wilfred E. *The Powers of the President: Problems of American Democracy.* Garden City, NJ: Doubleday, 1937.

Breckenridge, Adam C. *The Executive Privilege: Presidential Control over Information.* Lincoln: University of Nebraska Press, 1974.

Commager, Henry S. *The Defeat of America: Presidential Power and the National Character.* 2d ed. New York: Simon and Schuster, 1974.

Congressional Quarterly. *Powers of the Presidency.* Washington, DC: Congressional Quarterly, 1989.

Corwin, Edward S. *The President: Office and Power.* 5th ed. Revised by R. W. Bland et al. New York: New York University Press, 1984.

————. *Presidential Power and the Constitution: Essays.* Edited by Richard Loss. Ithaca, NY: Cornell University Press, 1976.

————. *President's Removal Power under the Constitution.* New York: National Municipal League, 1927.

Franklin, Daniel P. *Extraordinary Measures: The Exercise of Prerogative Powers in the United States.* Pittsburgh: University of Pittsburgh Press, 1991.

Hardin, Charles M. *Presidential Power and Accountability: Toward a New Constitution.* Chicago: University of Chicago Press, 1974.

Hargrove, Erwin C. *The Power of the Modern Presidency.* New York: Knopf, 1974.

Hart, John. *The Presidential Branch.* New York: Pergamon Press, 1987.

Hersh, Seymour M. *A View of the White House: A Study of Presidential Power.* New York: Macmillan, 1962.

Hirschfield, Robert S., comp. *The Power of the Presidency.* 3d ed. Chicago: Aldine Press, 1982.

Jackson, Carlton L. *Presidential Vetoes, 1792–1945.* Athens: University of Georgia Press, 1967.

Janis, Irving L. *Groupthink.* 2d. ed. Boston: Houghton Mifflin, 1982.

Lowi, Theodore J. *The Personal President: Power Invested, Promise Unfulfilled.* Ithaca, NY: Cornell University Press, 1985.

Mansfield, Harvey C. *Taming the Prince: The Ambivalence of Modern Executive Power.* New York: Free Press, 1989.

Milton, George F. *The Use of Presidential Power, 1789–1943.* Boston: Little, Brown, 1944.

Neustadt, Richard E. *Presidential Power and the Modern Presidents: The Politics of Leadership from Roosevelt to Reagan.* New York: Free Press, 1990.

Orman, John M. *Presidential Accountability: New and Recurring Issues.* Westport, CT: Greenwood Press, 1990.

————. *Presidential Secrecy and Deception: Beyond the Power to Persuade.* Westport, CT: Greenwood Press, 1980.

Pfiffner, James P. *The Managerial Presidency.* Pacific Grove, CA: Brooks/ Cole, 1989.

————. *The President, the Budget, and Congress: Impoundment and the 1974 Budget Act.* Boulder, CO: Westview Press, 1979.

Roche, John P., and Leonard W. Levy. *The Presidency.* New York: Harcourt Brace, 1964.

Sorenson, Theodore C. *Watchman in the Night: Presidential Accountability and Watergate.* Cambridge, MA: MIT Press, 1975.

Spitzer, Robert J. *The Presidential Veto: Touchstone of the American Presidency.* Ithaca: State University of New York Press, 1988.

Strum, Philippa. *Presidential Power and American Democracy,* 2d ed. Santa Monica, CA: Goodyear, 1979.

Stuckey, Mary E. *The President as Interpreter–in–Chief.* Chatham, NJ: Chatham House, 1991.

Warren, Sidney. *The President as World Leader.* New York: McGraw-Hill, 1967.

Watson, Richard A. *Presidential Vetoes and Public Policy.* Lawrence: University Press of Kansas, 1993.

Presidential Leadership

Barber, James D. *Political Leadership in American Government.* Boston: Little, Brown, 1964.

Burns, James M. *The Power to Lead: The Crisis of the American Presidency.* New York: Simon and Schuster, 1984.

———. *Presidential Government: The Crucible of Leadership.* Boston: Houghton Mifflin, 1973.

Davis, James W. *The President as Party Leader.* New York: Praeger, 1992.

Edwards, George C., III, and Stephen J. Wayne. *Presidential Leadership: Politics and Policy Making.* 3d ed. New York: St. Martin's Press, 1994.

Genovese, Michael A. *The Presidency in an Age of Limits.* Westport, CT: Greenwood Press, 1993.

Harmel, Robert, ed. *Presidents and Their Parties: Leadership or Neglect?* New York: Praeger, 1984.

Kernell, Samuel. *Going Public: New Strategies of Presidential Leadership.* 2d ed. Washington DC: CQ Press, 1993.

Kessler, Frank. *The Dilemmas of Presidential Leadership: Of Caretakers and Kings.* Englewood Cliffs, NJ: Prentice-Hall, 1982.

Milkis, Sidney M. *The President and the Parties: The Transformation of the American Party System since the New Deal.* New York: Oxford University Press, 1993.

Neustadt, Richard E. *Presidential Power: The Politics of Leadership from FDR to Carter.* New York: Wiley, 1980.

Ragsdale, Lyn. *Presidential Politics.* Boston: Houghton Mifflin, 1993.

Rockman, Bert A. *The Leadership Question: The Presidency and the American System.* New York: Praeger, 1984.

———. *The Myth of Leadership: The Presidency in the American System.* New York: Praeger, 1983.

Skowronek, Stephen. *The Politics Presidents Make: Leadership from John Adams to George Bush.* Cambridge, MA: Belknap Press, 1993.

Presidential Character

Bailey, Thomas A. *The Pugnacious Presidents: White House Warriors on Parade.* New York: Free Press, 1980.

Barber, James D. *The Presidential Character: Predicting Performance in the White House.* 4th ed. Englewood Cliffs, NJ: Prentice-Hall, 1992.

Buchanan, Bruce. *The Presidential Experience: What the Office Does to the Man.* Englewood Cliffs, NJ: Prentice Hall, 1978.

Campbell, Karlyn Kohrs, and Kathleen H. Jamieson. *Deeds Done in Words: Presidential Rhetoric and the Genres of Governance.* Chicago: University of Chicago Press, 1990.

Clark, James C. *Faded Glory: Presidents Out of Power.* New York: Praeger, 1985.

Cunningham, Noble E. *Popular Images of the Presidency: From Washington to Lincoln.* Columbia: University of Missouri Press, 1991.

Hargrove, Erwin C. *Presidential Leadership: Personality and Political Style.* New York: Macmillan, 1966.

Hutcheson, Richard G., Jr. *God in the White House: How Religion Has Changed the Modern Presidency.* New York: Macmillan, 1988.

Miller, Hope R. *Scandals in the Highest Office: Facts and Fictions in the Private Lives of Our Presidents.* New York: Random House, 1973.

Pessen, Edward. *The Log Cabin Myth: The Social Backgrounds of the Presidents.* New Haven, CT: Yale University Press, 1984.

The President and the Executive Branch

Hess, Stephen. *Organizing the Presidency.* Rev. ed. Washington, DC: Brookings Institution, 1988.

Kerbel, Matthew R. *Beyond Persuasion: Organizational Efficiency and Presidential Power.* Albany: State University of New York Press, 1991.

King, Anthony. *Both Ends of the Avenue: The Presidency, the Executive Branch, and Congress in the 1980's.* Washington, DC: American Enterprise Institute for Public Policy Research, 1983.

Pfiffner, James P., and R. Gordon Hoxie. *The Presidency in Transition.* New York: Center for the Study of the Presidency, 1989.

Thomas, Norman C., Hans W. Baade, and John C. Weistart, eds. *The Institutionalized Presidency.* Dobbs Ferry, NY: Oceana, 1972.

Tugwell, Rexford G. *The Enlargement of the Presidency.* Garden City, NY: Doubleday, 1960.

Wise, Sidney, and Richard F. Schier. *The Presidential Office.* New York: Crowell, 1968.

The Cabinet

Congressional Quarterly. *Cabinets and Counselors: The President and the Executive Branch.* Washington, DC: Congressional Quarterly, 1989.

Horn, Stephen S. *The Cabinet and Congress.* New York: Columbia University Press, 1960.

Learned, Henry B. *The President's Cabinet: Studies in the Origin, Formation, and Structure of an American Institution.* New Haven, CT: Yale University Press, 1927.

The White House Staff

Burke, John P. *The Institutional Presidency.* Baltimore: Johns Hopkins University Press, 1992.

Johnson, Richard T. *Managing the White House: An Intimate Study of the Presidency.* New York: Harper and Row, 1974.

McCormick, Thomas J., and Walter LaFeber, eds. *Behind the Throne: Servants of Power to Imperial Presidents, 1898–1968*. Madison: University of Wisconsin Press, 1993.

Patterson, Bradley H., Jr. *The Ring of Power: The White House Staff and Its Expanding Role in Government*. New York: Basic Books, 1988.

Sander, Alfred D. *A Staff for the President: The Executive Office, 1921–1952*. New York: Greenwood Press, 1989.

Witherspoon, Patricia D. *Within These Walls: A Study of Communication between Presidents and Their Senior Staffs*. New York: Praeger, 1991.

The White House Advisors

Cronin, Thomas E., and Sanford D. Greenberg. *The Presidential Advisory System*. New York: Harper and Row, 1969.

Flash, Edward S., Jr. *Economic Advice and Presidential Leadership: The Council of Economic Advisers*. New York: Columbia University Press, 1965.

Golden, William T. *Science Advice to the President*. 2d ed. Washington, DC: AAAS Press, 1992.

Koenig, Louis W. *The Invisible Presidency*. New York: Holt, 1960.

Marcy, Carl M. *Presidential Commissions*. New York: King's Crown Press, 1945.

Popper, Frank. *The President's Commissions*. New York: Twentieth Century Fund, 1970.

Wolanin, Thomas R. *The Presidential Advisory Commissions: Truman to Nixon*. Madison: University of Wisconsin Press, 1975.

The Vice Presidency

Barzman, Sol. *Madmen and Geniuses: The Vice-Presidents of the United States*. Chicago: Follett, 1974.

Dorman, Michael. *The Second Man: The Changing Role of the Vice President*. New York: Dell, 1970.

Goldstein, Joel K. *The Modern American Vice-Presidency: The Transformation of a Political Institution.* Princeton, NJ: Princeton University Press, 1982.

Nelson, Michael. *A Heartbeat Away: Report of the Twentieth Century Fund Task Force on the Vice Presidency.* New York: Priority Press Publications, 1988.

Witcover, Jules. *Crapshoot: Rolling the Dice on the Vice-Presidency.* New York: Crown, 1992.

Management of the Bureaucracy

Arnold, Peri E. *Making the Managerial Presidency: Comprehensive Reorganization Planning, 1905–1980.* Princeton, NJ: Princeton University Press, 1986.

Davis, James W. *The National Executive Branch.* New York: Free Press, 1970.

Gawthrop, Louis C. *Bureaucratic Behavior in the Executive Branch.* New York: Free Press, 1969.

Nathan, Richard P. *The Administrative Presidency.* New York: Wiley, 1983.

Policymaking

Allison, Graham T. *The Essence of Decision: Explaining the Cuban Missile Crisis.* Boston: Little, Brown, 1971.

Edwards, George C., III, Steven A. Shull, and Norman C. Thomas. *The Presidency and Public Policy Making.* Pittsburgh: University of Pittsburgh Press, 1985.

King, Gary, and Lyn Ragsdale. *The Elusive Executive: Discovering Statistical Patterns in the Presidency.* Washington, DC: CQ Press, 1988.

Rose, Richard. *Managing Presidential Objectives.* New York: Free Press, 1976.

Shull, Steven A. *Presidential Policy Making: An Analysis.* Brunswick, OH: King's Court Communications, 1979.

Shull, Steven A., and Lance T. LeLoup, eds. *Presidency: Studies in Public Policy.* Brunswick, OH: King's Court Communications, 1979.

Sorensen, Theodore C. *Decision Making in the White House.* New York: Columbia University Press, 1963.

Spitzer, Robert J. *The Presidency and Public Policy: The Four Arenas of Presidential Power.* University: University of Alabama Press, 1983.

Wildavsky, Aaron B., and Jeffrey L. Pressman. *Implementation.* 3d ed. Berkeley: University of California Press, 1984.

The President and Foreign Policy

Abshire, David M. *Foreign Policy Makers: President vs. Congress.* Beverly Hills, CA: Sage Publications, 1979.

Barilleaux, Ryan J. *The President and Foreign Affairs: Evaluation, Performance, and Power.* New York: Praeger, 1985.

Bostdorff, Denise M. *The Presidency and the Rhetoric of Foreign Crisis.* Columbia: University of South Carolina Press, 1994.

Corwin, Edward S. *The President's Control of Foreign Relations.* Princeton, NJ: Princeton University Press, 1917.

Crabb, Cecil V., Jr., and Pat M. Holt. *Invitation to Struggle: Congress, the President, and Foreign Policy.* 4th ed. Washington, DC: CQ Press, 1992.

Crabb, Cecil V., Jr., and Kevin V. Mulcahy. *Presidents and Foreign Policy Making: FDR to Reagan.* Baton Rouge: Louisiana State University Press, 1987.

Dawson, Joseph G., ed. *Commanders in Chief: Presidential Leadership in Modern Wars.* Lawrence: University Press of Kansas, 1993.

Destler, Irving M. *Presidents, Bureaucrats, and Foreign Policy: The Politics of Organizational Reform.* Princeton, NJ: Princeton University Press, 1972.

Fleming, Denna F. *The Treaty Veto of the American Senate.* New York: G. P. Putnam's Sons, 1930.

Furlong, William L., and Margaret E. Scranton. *The Dynamics of Foreign Policymaking: The President, the Congress, and the Panama Canal Treaties.* Boulder, CO: Westview Press, 1984.

George, Alexander L. *Presidential Decision Making in Foreign Policy: The Effective Use of Information and Advice.* Boulder, CO: Westview Press, 1980.

Glennon, Michael J. *Constitutionality Diplomacy.* Princeton, NJ: Princeton University Press, 1990.

Graber, Doris A. *Public Opinion, the President, and Foreign Policy: Four Case Studies from the Formative Years.* New York: Holt, Rinehart and Winston, 1968.

Hassler, Warren W. *The President as Commander in Chief.* Reading, MA: Addison-Wesley, 1971.

Holt, William S. *Treaties Defeated by the Senate: A Study of the Struggle between President and Senate over the Conduct of Foreign Relations.* Baltimore: Johns Hopkins University Press, 1933.

Hunter, Robert E. *Presidential Control of Foreign Policy.* New York: Praeger, 1992.

Hybel, Alex R. *Power over Rationality: The Bush Administration and the Gulf Crisis.* Ithaca: State University of New York Press, 1993.

Kellerman, Barbara, and Ryan J. Barilleaux. *The President as World Leader.* New York: St. Martin's Press, 1991.

Lehman, John. *The Executive, Congress, and Foreign Policy.* New York: Praeger, 1976.

Mann, Thomas E., ed. *A Question of Balance: The President, the Congress, and Foreign Policy.* Washington, DC: Brookings Institution, 1990.

Nuechterlein, Donald E. *National Interests and Presidential Leadership.* Boulder, CO: Westview Press, 1978.

Rieselbach, Leroy N. *The Roots of Isolationism: Congressional Voting and Presidential Leadership in Foreign Policy.* Indianapolis: Bobbs-Merrill, 1966.

Rourke, John T. *Congress and the Presidency in U.S. Foreign Policymaking: A Study of Interaction and Influence, 1945–1982.* Boulder, CO: Westview Press, 1983.

Spanier, John, and Joseph Nogee, eds. *Congress, the Presidency, and American Foreign Policy.* New York: Pergamon Press, 1981.

Wilcox, Francis O. *Congress, the Executive, and Foreign Policy.* New York: Harper and Row, 1971.

War-Making Powers

Caraley, Demetrios, ed. *The President's War Powers: From the Federalists to Reagan.* New York: Academy of Political Science, 1984.

Grundstein, Nathan D. *Presidential Delegation of Authority in Wartime.* Pittsburgh: University of Pittsburgh Press, 1961.

Javits, Jacob K. *Who Makes War: The President versus Congress.* New York: William Morrow and Company, 1973.

Lehman, John F. *Making War: The 200-Year-Old Battle between the President and Congress over How America Goes to War.* New York: Scribner's, 1992.

Reveley, W. Taylor, III. *War Powers of the President and Congress: Who Holds the Arrows and Olive Branch?* Charlottesville: University of Virginia Press, 1981.

Whicker, Marcia L., James P. Pfiffner, and Raymond A. Moore. *The Presidency and the Persian Gulf War.* Westport, CT: Praeger, 1993.

Whiting, William. *The War Powers of the President.* Boston: Houghton Mifflin, 1984.

Wormuth, Francis D., and Edwin B. Firmage. *To Chain the Dog of War: The War Power of Congress in History and Law.* Dallas: Southern Methodist University Press, 1986.

Executive Agreements

Johnson, Loch K. *The Making of International Agreements: Congress Confronts the Executive.* New York: New York University Press, 1984.

Margolis, Lawrence S. *Executive Agreements and Presidential Power in Foreign Policy.* New York: Praeger, 1985.

Millett, Stephen M. *The Constitutionality of Executive Agreements: United States v. Belmont.* New York: Garland Publishing, 1990.

National Security Policy

Crabb, Cecil V., Jr., and Kevin V. Mulcahy. *American National Security: A Presidential Perspective.* Pacific Grove, CA: Brooks/Cole, 1991.

Hoxie, R. Gordon, ed. *The Presidency and National Security.* New York: Center for the Study of the Presidency, 1984.

Keynes, Edward. *Undeclared War: Twilight Zone of Constitutional Power.* University Park: Pennsylvania State University Press, 1982.

Sarkesian, Sam C., ed. *Presidential Leadership and National Security: Style, Institutions, and Politics.* Boulder, CO: Westview Press, 1984.

The President and Domestic Policy

Amaker, Norman C. *Civil Rights and the Reagan Administration.* Washington, DC: Urban Institute Press, 1988.

Berman, Larry. *The Office of Management and Budget and the Presidency, 1921–1979.* Princeton, NJ: Princeton University Press, 1979.

Durant, Robert F. *The Administrative Presidency Revisited: Public Lands, the BLM, and the Reagan Revolution.* Ithaca: State University of New York Press, 1992.

Fisher, Louis. *Presidential Spending Power.* Princeton, NJ: Princeton University Press, 1975.

Katz, James E. *Presidential Politics and Science Policy.* New York: Praeger, 1978.

Kessel, John H. *The Domestic Presidency: Decision–Making in the White House.* North Scituate, MA: Duxbury Press, 1975.

Larkin, John D. *The President's Control of the Tariff.* Cambridge, MA: Harvard University Press 1936.

Light, Paul C. *The President's Agenda: Domestic Policy Choice from Kennedy to Carter.* Rev. ed. Baltimore: Johns Hopkins University Press, 1991.

McQuaid, Kim. *Big Business and Presidential Power: From FDR to Reagan.* New York: William Morrow and Company, 1982.

Shull, Steven A. *Domestic Policy Formation: Presidential–Congressional Partnership?* Westport, CT: Greenwood Press, 1983.

————. *The President and Civil Rights Policy: Leadership and Change.* New York: Greenwood Press, 1989.

Stein, Herbert. *Presidential Economics: The Making of Economic Policy from Roosevelt to Clinton.* 3d ed. New York: American Enterprise Institute for Public Policy Research, 1994.

The President and Congress

Binkley, Wilfred E. *The President and Congress.* 3d ed. New York: Vintage, 1962.

Black, Henry C. *The Relation of the Executive Power to Legislation.* Princeton, NJ: Princeton University Press, 1919.

Bond, Jon R., and Richard Fleisher. *The President in the Legislative Arena.* Chicago: University of Chicago Press, 1990.

Bowles, Nigel. *The White House and Capitol Hill: The Politics of Presidential Persuasion.* New York: Oxford University Press, 1987.

Chamberlain, Lawrence H. *The President, Congress, and Legislation.* New York: Columbia University Press, 1946.

Davis, James W., and Delbert Ringquist. *The President and Congress: Toward a New Balance.* Woodbury, NY: Barron's Educational Series, 1975.

Edwards, George C., III. *At the Margins: Presidential Leadership of Congress.* New Haven, CT: Yale University Press, 1989.

————. *Presidential Influence in Congress.* San Francisco: W. H. Freeman, 1980.

Fisher, Louis. *The Politics of Shared Power: Congress and the Executive.* 3d ed. Washington, DC; CQ Press, 1993.

———. *President and Congress: Power and Policy.* New York: Free Press, 1972.

Franck, Thomas M., ed. *The Tethered Presidency: Congressional Restraints on Executive Power.* New York: New York University Press, 1981.

Harris, Joseph P. *The Advice and Consent of the Senate: A Study of the Confirmation of Appointments by the United States Senate.* Berkeley: University of California Press, 1953.

Herring, Edward P. *Presidential Leadership: The Political Relations of Congress and the Chief Executive.* New York: Farrar and Rinehardt, 1940.

Hunter, Robert E., Wayne L. Berman, and John F. Kennedy. *Making Government Work: From White House to Congress.* Boulder, CO: Westview Press, 1986.

Johannes, John R. *Policy Innovation in Congress.* Morristown, NJ: General Learning Press, 1972.

Koenig, Louis W. *Congress and the President: Official Makers of Public Policy.* Glenview, IL: Scott, Foresman, 1965.

LeLoup, Lance T. *Congress and the President: The Policy Connection.* Belmont, CA: Wadsworth, 1993.

Livingston, William S., Lawrence C. Dodd, and Richard L. Schott, eds. *The Presidency and the Congress: A Shifting Balance of Power.* Austin: Lyndon B. Johnson School of Public Affairs, University of Texas, 1979.

Maass, Arthur. *Congress and the Common Good.* New York: Basic Books, 1983.

Mackenzie, George C. *The Politics of Presidential Appointments.* New York: Free Press, 1981.

Mansfield, Harvey C., ed. *Congress against the President.* New York: Praeger, 1975.

Marini, John A. *The Politics of Budget Control: Congress, the Presidency, and the Growth of the Administrative State.* Washington, DC: Crane Russak, 1992.

Mayhew, David R. *Divided We Govern: Party Control, Lawmaking, and Investigations, 1946–1990.* New Haven, CT: Yale University Press, 1991.

Mezey, Michael L. *Congress, the President, and Public Policy.* Boulder, CO: Westview Press, 1989.

Moe, Ronald C., ed. *Congress and the President: Allies and Adversaries.* Pacific Palisades, CA: Goodyear, 1971.

Parker, Glenn R. *Political Beliefs about the Structure of Government: Congress and the Presidency.* Beverly Hills, CA: Sage Publications, 1974.

Peterson, Mark A. *Legislating Together: The White House and Capitol Hill from Eisenhower to Reagan.* Cambridge, MA: Harvard University Press, 1990.

Polsby, Nelson W. *Congress and the Presidency.* 4th ed. Englewood Cliffs, NJ: Prentice–Hall, 1986.

———. *The President and Congress.* Englewood Cliffs, NJ: Prentice-Hall, 1964.

Pyle, Christopher H., and Richard M. Pious. *The President, Congress, and the Constitution.* New York: Free Press, 1984.

Schlesinger, Arthur M., Jr., and Alfred DeGrazia. *Congress and the Presidency: Their Role in Modern Times.* Washington, DC: American Enterprise Institute for Public Policy Research, 1967.

Shull, Steven A., ed. *The Two Presidencies: A Quarter Century Assessment.* Chicago: Nelson-Hall, 1991.

Shuman, Howard E. *Politics and the Budget: The Struggle between the President and the Congress.* 3d ed. Englewood Cliffs, NJ: Prentice-Hall, 1992.

Spitzer, Robert J. *President and Congress: Executive Hegemony at the Crossroads of American Government.* Philadelphia: Temple University Press, 1993.

Thurber, James A., ed. *Divided Democracy: Cooperation and Conflict between the President and Congress.* Washington, DC: CQ Press, 1991.

Wayne, Stephen J. *The Legislative Presidency.* New York: Harper and Row, 1978.

The President and the Judiciary

Abraham, Henry J. *Justices and Presidents: Political History of Appointments of the Supreme Courts.* 3d ed. New York: Oxford University Press, 1992.

Caplan, Lincoln. *The Tenth Justice: The Solicitor General and the Rule of Law.* New York: Knopf, 1987.

Massaro, John. *Supremely Political: The Role of Ideology and Presidential Management in Unsuccessful Supreme Court Nominations.* Albany: State University of New York Press, 1990.

Rossiter, Clinton L. *The Supreme Court and the Commander in Chief.* Rev. ed. Ithaca, NY: Cornell University Press, 1976.

Schubert, Glendon A. *The Presidency in the Courts.* Minneapolis: University of Minnesota Press, 1957.

Scigliano, Robert. *The Supreme Court and the Presidency.* New York: Free Press, 1971.

Presidential Media Coverage

Cornwell, Elmer E., Jr. *The Presidency and the Press.* Morristown, NJ: General Learning Press, 1974.

―――. *Presidential Leadership of Public Opinion.* Bloomington: Indiana University Press, 1965.

Denton, Robert E., and Dan F. Hahn. *Presidential Communications: Description and Analysis.* New York: Praeger, 1986

Forbath, Peter, and Carey Winfrey. *The Adversaries: The President and the Press.* Cleveland, OH: King's Court Communications, 1974.

French, Blaire A. *The Presidential Press Conference: Its History and Role in the American Political System.* Washington, DC: University Press of America, 1982.

Grossman, Michael B., and Martha J. Kumar. *Portraying the President: The White House and the News Media.* Baltimore: Johns Hopkins University Press, 1981.

Juergens, George. *News from the White House: The Presidential-Press Relationship in the Progressive Era.* Chicago: University of Chicago Press, 1981.

Minow, Newton N., John B. Martin, and Lee M. Mitchell. *Presidential Television.* New York: Basic Books, 1973.

Morgan, Edward P., Max Ways, Clark Mollenhoff, Peter Lisagor, and Herbert G. Klein. *The Presidency and the Press Conference.* Washington, DC: American Enterprise Institute for Public Policy Research, 1971.

Purvis, Hoyt, ed. *The Presidency and the Press.* Austin: Lyndon B. Johnson School of Public Affairs, University of Texas, 1976.

Smith, Howard E. *Newsmakers: The Press and the Presidents.* Reading, MA: Addison-Wesley, 1974.

Spear, Joseph C. *Presidents and the Press: The Nixon Legacy.* Cambridge, MA: MIT Press, 1984.

Spragens, William C. *The Presidency and the Mass Media in the Age of Television.* Washington, DC: University Press of America, 1978.

Public Opinion of Presidents

Brace, Paul, and Barbara Hinckley. *Follow the Leader: Opinion Polls and the Modern Presidents.* New York: Basic Books, 1992.

Brody, Richard A. *Assessing the President: The Media, Elite Opinion, and Public Support.* Stanford, CA: Stanford University Press, 1991.

Edwards, George C., III. *The Public Presidency: The Pursuit of Popular Support.* New York: St. Martin's Press, 1983.

Lanoue, David J. *From Camelot to the Teflon President: Economics and Presidential Popularity since 1960.* New York: Greenwood Press, 1988.

Monroe, Kristen R. *Presidential Popularity and the Economy.* New York: Praeger, 1984.

Mueller, John E. *War, Presidents, and Public Opinion.* New York: Wiley, 1973.

The Selection of Presidents

Aldrich, John H. *Before the Convention: A Theory of Presidential Nomination Campaigns.* Chicago: University of Chicago Press, 1980.

Barber, James D. *Choosing the President.* Englewood Cliffs, NJ: Prentice-Hall, 1974.

Berelson, Bernard, Paul F. Lazarsfeld, and William N. McPhee. *Voting: A Study of Opinion Formation in a Presidential Campaign.* Chicago: University of Chicago Press, 1954.

Boller, Paul F., Jr. *Presidential Campaigns.* New York: Oxford University Press, 1984.

Buchanan, Bruce. *Electing a President: The Markle Commission Research on Campaign '88.* Austin: University of Texas Press, 1991.

Ceaser, James W. *Presidential Selection: Theory and Development.* Princeton, NJ: Princeton University Press, 1979.

———. *Reforming the Reforms: A Critical Analysis of the Presidential Selection Process.* Cambridge, MA: Ballinger, 1982.

Euchner, Charles C., and John A. Maltese. *Selecting the President: From Washington to Bush.* Washington, DC: Congressional Quarterly, 1992.

Fishel, Jeff. *Presidents and Promises: From Campaign Pledge to Presidential Performance.* Washington, DC: CQ Press, 1985.

Heard, Alexander, and Michael Nelson, eds. *Presidential Selection.* Durham, NC: Duke University Press, 1987.

Hess, Stephen. *Presidential Campaign: Leadership Selection Process after Watergate: Essay.* Rev. ed. Washington, DC: Brookings Institution, 1978.

Jamieson, Kathleen H. *Packaging the Presidency: A History and Criticism of Advertising.* 2d ed. New York: Oxford University Press, 1992.

Kessel, John H. *Presidential Campaign Politics.* 4th ed. Pacific Grove, CA: Brooks/Cole, 1992.

———. *Presidential Parties.* Homewood, IL: Dorsey Press, 1984.

Key, Valdimer O. *Politics, Parties, and Pressure Groups.* 5th ed. New York: Crowell, 1964.

Lengle, James I., and Byron E. Shafer, eds. *Presidential Politics: Readings on Nominations and Elections.* New York: St. Martin's Press, 1980.

Miller, Warren F., and M. Kent Jennings. *Parties in Transition: A Longitudinal Study of Party Elites and Supporters.* New York: Russell Sage Foundation, 1986.

Newman, Bruce I. *The Marketing of the President: Political Marketing as Campaign Strategy.* Thousand Oaks, CA: Sage Publications, 1994.

Nie, Norman H., Sidney Verba, and John R. Petrocik. *The Changing American Voter.* Enlarged ed. Cambridge, MA: Harvard University Press, 1979.

Popkin, Samuel L. *The Reasoning Voter: Communication and Persuasion in Presidential Campaigns.* 2d ed. Chicago: University of Chicago Press, 1994.

Reiter, Howard L. *Selecting the President: The Nominating Process in Transition.* Philadelphia: University of Pennsylvania Press, 1985.

Rose, Gary L., ed. *Controversial Issues in Presidential Selection.* 2d ed. Albany: State University of New York Press, 1994.

Russell, Francis. *The President Makers: From Mark Hanna to Joseph P. Kennedy.* Boston: Little, Brown, 1976.

Smith, Eric. *The Unchanging American Voter.* Berkeley: University of California Press, 1989.

Taylor, Paul. *See How They Run: Electing a President in an Age of Mediaocracy.* New York: Knopf, 1990.

Wattenberg, Martin P. *The Rise of Candidate-Centered Politics: Presidential Elections in the 1980s.* Cambridge, MA: Harvard University Press, 1991.

Primaries

Bartels, Larry M. *Presidential Primaries and the Dynamics of Public Choice.* Princeton, NJ: Princeton University Press, 1988.

Crotty, William J., and John S. Jackson. *Presidential Primaries and Nominations.* Washington, DC: CQ Press, 1985.

Davis, James W. *Presidential Primaries: The Road to the White House.* Westport, CT: Greenwood Press, 1980.

————. *Springboard to the White House: Presidential Primaries: How They Are Fought and Won.* New York: Crowell, 1967.

Geer, John G. *Nominating Presidents: An Evaluation of Voters and Primaries.* Westport, CT: Greenwood Press, 1989.

Conventions

Bain, Richard, and Judith H. Parris. *Convention Decisions and Voting Records.* 2d ed. Washington, DC: Brookings Institution, 1973.

Chase, James S. *Emergence of the Presidential Nominating Conventions, 1789–1832.* Urbana: University of Illinois Press, 1973.

David, Paul T., Ralph M. Goldman, and Richard D. Baia. *The Politics of National Party Conventions.* Rev. ed. New York: Random House, 1984.

Parris, Judith H. *The Convention Problem: Issues in Reform of Presidential Nominating Procedure.* Washington, DC: Brookings Institution, 1972.

Pomper, Gerald M. *Nominating the President: The Politics of Convention Choice, With a New Postscript on 1964.* New York: W. W. Norton, 1966.

Shafer, Byron E. *Bifurcated Politics: Evolution and Reform in the National Party Convention.* Cambridge, MA: Harvard University Press, 1988.

Campaign Debates

Bishop, George F., Robert G. Meadow, and Marilyn Jackson-Beeck. *Presidential Debates: Media, Electoral, and Policy Perspectives*. New York: Praeger, 1978.

Hinck, Edward A. *Enacting the Presidency: Political Argument, Presidential Debates, and Presidential Character*. Westport, CT: Praeger, 1993.

Jamieson, Kathleen H., and David S. Birdsell. *Presidential Debates: The Challenge of Creating an Informed Electorate*. New York: Oxford University Press, 1988.

Lanoue, David J., and Peter R. Schrott. *The Joint Press Conference: The History, Impact, and Prospects of American Presidential Debates*. New York: Greenwood Press, 1991.

Minow, Newton N., and Clifford M. Sloan. *For Great Debates: A New Plan for Future Presidential TV Debates*. New York: Priority Press Publications, 1987.

Ranney, Austin, ed. *The Past and Future of Presidential Debates*. Washington, DC: American Enterprise Institute for Public Policy Research, 1979.

Swerdlow, Joel L. *Beyond Debate: A Paper on Televised Presidential Debates*. New York: Twentieth Century Fund, 1984.

Campaign Finances

Alexander, Herbert E. *Financing Politics: Money, Elections, and Political Reform*. 4th ed. Washington, DC: CQ Press, 1992.

———. *Money in Politics*. Washington, DC: Public Affairs Press, 1972.

Dunn, Delmer D. *Financing Presidential Campaigns*. Washington, DC: Brookings Institution, 1972.

———. *Paying for Politics: Highlights of Financing Presidential Campaigns*. Washington, DC: Brookings Institution, 1972.

The Media and Presidential Selection

Arterton, F. Christopher. *Media Politics: The News Strategies of Presidential Campaigns*. Lexington, MA: Lexington Books, 1984.

Barber, James D. *The Pulse of Politics: Electing Presidents in the Media Age.* New York: W. W. Norton, 1980.

————. *Race for the Presidency: The Media and the Nominating Process.* Englewood Cliffs, NJ: Prentice-Hall, 1978.

Foley, John, Dennis A. Britton, and Eugene B. Everett, Jr. *Nominating a President: The Process and the Press.* New York: Praeger, 1980.

McCubbins, Mathew D., ed. *Under the Watchful Eye: Managing Presidential Campaigns in the Television Era.* Washington, DC: CQ Press, 1992.

Morreale, Joanne. *The Presidential Campaign Film: A Critical History.* Westport, CT: Praeger, 1993.

Patterson, Thomas E. *The Mass Media Election: How Americans Choose Their President.* New York: Praeger, 1980.

Weaver, David H., Doris A. Graber, M. E. McCombs, and C. H. Eyal. *Media Agenda-Setting in a Presidential Election: Issues, Images, and Interest.* New York: Praeger, 1981.

Voting in Presidential Elections

Asher, Herbert B. *Presidential Elections and American Politics: Voters, Candidates, and Campaigns since 1952.* 5th ed. Pacific Grove, CA: Brooks/Cole, 1992.

Black, Earl, and Merle Black. *The Vital South: How Presidents Are Elected.* Cambridge, MA: Harvard University Press, 1992.

Burnham, Walter D. *Critical Elections and the Mainsprings of American Politics.* New York: W. W. Norton, 1970.

Campbell, James E. *The Presidential Pulse of Congressional Elections.* Lexington: University Press of Kentucky, 1993.

Cantor, Robert D. *Voting Behavior and Presidential Elections.* Itasca, IL: F. E. Peacock, 1975.

Cummings, Milton C., Jr. *Congressman and the Electorate: Elections for the U.S. House and President, 1920–1964.* New York: Free Press, 1966.

Fiorina, Morris P. *Retrospective Voting Behavior in American National Elections.* New Haven, CT: Yale University Press, 1981.

Flanigan, William H. *Electoral Behavior.* Boston: Little, Brown, 1969.

Flanigan, William H., and Zingale, Nancy H. *Political Behavior of the American Electorate.* 8th ed. Washington, DC: CQ Press, 1994.

Key, Valdimer O., and Milton C. Cummings. *The Responsible Electorate: Rationality in Presidential Voting, 1936–1960.* Cambridge, MA: Harvard University Press, 1966.

Lazarsfeld, Paul F., Bernard Berelson, and Hazel Gaudet. *The People's Choice: How the Voter Makes up His Mind in a Presidential Campaign.* 3d ed. New York: Columbia University Press, 1968.

Moos, Malcolm. *Politics, Presidents, and Coattails.* Baltimore: Johns Hopkins University Press, 1952.

Page, Benjamin I. *Choices and Echos in Presidential Elections: Rational Man and Electoral Democracy.* Chicago: University of Chicago Press, 1978.

Patterson, Thomas E. *Out of Order.* New York: Knopf, 1993.

Pious, Richard M., ed. *Presidents, Elections, and Democracy.* New York: Academy of Political Science, 1992.

Schlesinger, Arthur M., Jr., and Fred L. Israel, eds. *The Coming to Power: Critical Presidential Elections in American History.* New York: Chelsea House, 1972.

The Electoral College

Berns, Walter, ed. *After the People Vote: A Guide to the Electoral College.* Rev. ed. Washington, DC: AEI Press, 1992.

Best, Judith V. *The Case against Direct Election of the President: A Defense of the Electoral College.* Ithaca, NY: Cornell University Press, 1975.

Bickel, Alexander M. *Reform and Continuity: The Electoral College, the Convention, and the Party System.* New York: Harper and Row, 1971.

Diamond, Martin. *The Electoral College and the American Idea of Democracy.* Washington, DC: American Enterprise Institute for Public Policy Research, 1977.

Glennon, Michael J. *When No Majority Rules: The Electoral College and Presidential Succession.* Washington, DC: CQ Press, 1993.

Peirce, Neal R. *The People's President: The Electoral College in American History and the Direct Vote Alternative.* New York: Simon and Schuster, 1968.

Peirce, Neal R., and Lawrence D. Longley. *The People's President: The Electoral College in American History and the Direct Vote Alternative.* Rev. ed. New Haven, CT: Yale University Press, 1981.

Sayre, Wallace S., and Judith H. Parris. *Voting for President: The Electoral College and the American Political System.* Washington, DC: Brookings Institution, 1970.

Wilmerding, Lucius, Jr. *The Electoral College.* New Brunswick, NJ: Rutgers University Press, 1958.

Zeidenstein, Harvey G. *Direct Election of the President.* Lexington, MA: Lexington Books, 1973.

Presidential Election Studies

Brams, Steven J. *The Presidential Election Game.* New Haven, CT: Yale University Press, 1978.

Burnham, Walter D. *Presidential Ballots, 1836–1892.* Baltimore: Johns Hopkins University Press, 1955.

Ewing, Cortez A. *Presidential Elections from Abraham Lincoln to Franklin D. Roosevelt.* Norman: University of Oklahoma Press, 1940.

Mazmanian, Daniel A. *Third Parties in Presidential Elections.* Washington, DC: Brookings Institution, 1974.

Miller, Warren E., and Teresa E. Levitin. *Leadership and Change: Presidential Elections from 1952 to 1976.* Cambridge, MA: Winthrop, 1976.

Polsby, Nelson W., and Aaron B. Wildavsky. *Presidential Elections.* 8th ed. New York: Scribner's, 1992.

Roseboom, Eugene H., and Alfred E. Eckes. *A History of Presidential Elections, From George Washington to Jimmy Carter.* 4th ed. New York: Macmillan, 1979.

Schlesinger, Arthur M., Jr., and Fred L. Israel. *History of American Presidential Elections, 1789–1984.* 10 vols. New York: Chelsea House, 1985.

Watson, Richard A. *The Presidential Contest.* 4th ed. New York: Wiley, 1992.

Wayne, Stephen J. *The Road to the White House 1992: The Politics of Presidential Elections.* 4th ed. New York: St. Martin's Press, 1992.

White, Theodore H. *America in Search of Itself: The Making of the President 1956–1980.* New York: Harper and Row, 1982.

Presidential Transitions

Brauer, Carl M. *Presidential Transitions from Eisenhower through Reagan: Peril and Opportunity.* New York: Oxford University Press, 1986.

Germino, Dante L. *The Inaugural Addresses of American Presidents: The Public Philosophy and Rhetoric.* Lanham, MD: University Press of America, 1984.

Henry, Laurin L. *Presidential Transitions.* Washington, DC: Brookings Institution, 1960.

Lomask, Milton. *"I Do Solemnly Swear...," The Story of the Presidential Inauguration.* New York: Farrar, Straus, and Giroux, 1966.

Pfiffner, James P. *The Strategic Presidency: Hitting the Ground Running.* Chicago: Dorsey Press, 1988.

Presidential Succession

Bayh, Birch E. *One Heartbeat Away: Presidential Disability and Succession.* Indianapolis: Bobbs-Merrill, 1968.

Silva, Ruth C. *Presidential Succession.* Ann Arbor: University of Michigan Press, 1951.

Sindler, Allan P. *Unchosen Presidents: Vice President and Other Frustrations of Presidential Succession.* Berkeley: University of California Press, 1976.

The Presidents

George Washington

Ferling, John E. *The First of Men: A Life of George Washington*. Knoxville: University of Tennessee Press, 1988.

Flexner, James T. *George Washington and the New Nation*. Boston: Little, Brown, 1970.

———. *George Washington: Anguish and Farewell*. Boston: Little, Brown, 1969.

———. *George Washington in the American Revolution*. Boston: Little, Brown, 1968.

———. *Washington, the Indispensable Man*. Boston: Little, Brown, 1974.

Freeman, Douglas S. *George Washington: A Biography*. 7 vols. New York: Scribner's, 1948–1957.

Phelps, Glenn A. *George Washington and American Constitutionalism*. Lawrence: University Press of Kansas, 1993.

Smith, Richard N. *Patriarch: George Washington and the New American Nation*. Boston: Houghton Mifflin, 1993.

Wister, Owen. *The Seven Ages of Washington: A Bibliography*. New York: Macmillan, 1907.

John Adams

Adams, Charles F. *The Life of John Adams*. Rev. ed. 2 vols. Philadelphia: Lippincott, 1871.

Bowen, Catherine D. *John Adams and the American Revolution*. Boston: Little, Brown, 1950.

Brown, Ralph A. *The Presidency of John Adams*. Lawrence: Regents Press of Kansas, 1975.

Ellis, Joseph J. *Passionate Sage: The Character and Legacy of John Adams*. New York: W. W. Norton, 1993.

Ferling, John E. *John Adams: A Life.* Knoxville: University of Tennessee Press, 1992.

Kurtz, Stephen G. *The Presidency of John Adams: The Collapse of Federalism, 1795–1800.* Philadelphia: University of Pennsylvania Press, 1957.

Smith, Page. *John Adams.* 2 vols. Garden City, NY: Doubleday, 1962.

Thomas Jefferson

Brodie, Fawn M. *Thomas Jefferson: An Intimate History.* New York: W. W. Norton, 1974.

Cunningham, Noble E. *In Pursuit of Reason: The Life of Thomas Jefferson.* Baton Rouge: Louisiana State University Press, 1987.

———. *The Process of Government under Jefferson.* Princeton, NJ: Princeton University Press, 1978.

Fleming, Thomas J. *The Man from Monticello: An Intimate Life of Thomas Jefferson.* New York: William Morrow and Company, 1969.

Johnstone, Robert M., Jr. *Jefferson and the Presidency, Leadership in the Young Republic.* Ithaca, NY: Cornell University Press, 1978.

Malone, Dumas. *Jefferson and the Ordeal of Liberty.* Boston: Little, Brown, 1962.

———. *Jefferson the President: First Term, 1801–1805.* Boston: Little, Brown, 1970.

———. *Jefferson the President: Second Term, 1805–1809.* Boston: Little, Brown, 1974.

———. *Jefferson the Virginian.* Boston: Little, Brown, 1948.

———. *The Jeffersonian Heritage.* Boston: Beacon Press, 1953.

———. *The Sage of Monticello.* Boston: Little, Brown, 1981.

———. *Thomas Jefferson as a Political Leader.* Berkeley: University of California Press, 1963.

McDonald, Forrest. *The Presidency of Thomas Jefferson*. Lawrence: Regents Press of Kansas, 1976.

Peterson, Merrill D. *The Jefferson Image in the American Mind*. New York: Oxford University Press, 1960.

Randall, Willard S. *Thomas Jefferson: A Life*. New York: Holt, 1993.

Tucker, Robert W. *Empire of Liberty: The Statecraft of Thomas Jefferson*. New York: Oxford University Press, 1990.

James Madison

Brant, Irving. *James Madison*. 6 vols. Indianapolis: Bobbs-Merrill, 1941–1961.

Ketcham, Ralph L. *James Madison: A Biography*. New York: Macmillan, 1971.

Matthews, Richard K. *If Men Were Angels: James Madison and the Heartless Empire of Reason*. Lawrence: University Press of Kansas, 1995.

McCoy, Drew R. *The Last of the Fathers: James Madison and the Republican Legacy*. New York: Cambridge University Press, 1989.

Rakove, Jack N. *James Madison and the Creation of the American Republic*. New York: HarperCollins, 1990.

Rutland, Robert A. *The Presidency of James Madison*. Lawrence: University Press of Kansas, 1990.

James Monroe

Ammon, Harry. *James Monroe: The Quest for National Identity*. New York: McGraw-Hill, 1971.

Cresson, William P. *James Monroe*. Chapel Hill: University of North Carolina Press, 1946.

Dangerfield, George. *The Era of Good Feelings*. New York: Harcourt Brace, 1952.

May, Ernest R. *The Making of the Monroe Doctrine*. Cambridge, MA: Harvard University Press, 1975.

Wilmerding, Lucius, Jr. *James Monroe, Public Claimant.* New Brunswick, NJ: Rutgers University Press, 1960.

John Quincy Adams

Bemis, Samuel F. *John Quincy Adams and the Foundations of American Foreign Policy.* New York: Knopf, 1949.

————. *John Quincy Adams and the Union.* New York: Knopf, 1956.

Hecht, Marie B. *John Quincy Adams: A Personal History of an Independent Man.* New York: Macmillan, 1972.

Weeks, William Earl. *John Quincy Adams and American Global Empire.* Lexington: University Press of Kentucky, 1992.

Andrew Jackson

Cole, Donald B. *The Presidency of Andrew Jackson.* Lawrence: University Press of Kansas, 1993.

Curtis, James C. *Andrew Jackson and the Search for Vindication.* Boston: Little, Brown, 1976.

Latner, Richard B. *The Presidency of Andrew Jackson: White House Politics, 1829–1837.* Athens: University of Georgia Press, 1979.

Remini, Robert V. *The Age of Jackson.* Columbia: University of South Carolina Press, 1972.

————. *Andrew Jackson and the Course of American Democracy, 1833–1845.* New York: Harper and Row, 1984.

————. *Andrew Jackson and the Course of American Empire, 1767–1821.* New York: Harper and Row, 1977.

————. *Andrew Jackson and the Course of American Freedom: 1822–1832.* New York: Harper and Row, 1981.

————. *The Election of Andrew Jackson.* Philadelphia: Lippincott, 1963.

————. *The Life of Andrew Jackson.* New York: Harper and Row, 1988.

————. *The Revolutionary Age of Andrew Jackson.* New York: Harper and Row, 1976.

Schlesinger, Arthur M., Jr. *The Age of Jackson.* Boston: Little, Brown, 1945.

White, Leonard D. *The Jacksonians: A Study in Administrative History, 1829–1861.* New York: Macmillan, 1954.

Martin Van Buren

Cole, Donald B. *Martin Van Buren and the American Political System.* Princeton, NJ: Princeton University Press, 1984.

Curtis, James C. *The Fox at Bay: Martin Van Buren and the Presidency, 1837–1841.* Lexington: University of Kentucky Press, 1970.

Niven, John. *Martin Van Buren: The Romantic Age of American Politics.* New York: Oxford University Press, 1983.

Remini, Robert V. *Martin Van Buren and the Making of the Democratic Party.* New York: Columbia University Press, 1959.

Wilson, Major L. *The Presidency of Martin Van Buren.* Lawrence: University Press of Kansas, 1984.

William Henry Harrison

Cleaves, Freeman. *Old Tippecanoe: William Henry Harrison and His Time.* New York: Scribner's 1939.

Peckham, Howard H. *William Henry Harrison: Young Tippecanoe.* Indianapolis: Bobbs-Merrill, 1951.

Peterson, Norma L. *The Presidencies of William Henry Harrison & John Tyler.* Lawrence: University Press of Kansas, 1989.

John Tyler

Chitwood, Oliver P. *John Tyler: Champion of the Old South.* New York: Appleton, 1939.

Morgan, Robert J. *A Whig Embattled: The Presidency under John Tyler.* Lincoln: University of Nebraska Press, 1954.

Peterson, Norma L. *The Presidencies of William Henry Harrison & John Tyler.* Lawrence: University Press of Kansas, 1989.

Seager, Robert. *And Tyler Too: A Biography of John and Julia Gardiner Tyler.* New York: McGraw-Hill, 1963.

Young, Stanley P. *Tippecanoe and Tyler, Too!* New York: Random House, 1957.

James K. Polk

Bergeron, Paul H. *The Presidency of James K. Polk.* Lawrence: University Press of Kansas, 1987.

McCormac, Eugene I. *James K. Polk, A Political Biography.* Berkeley: University of California Press, 1922.

McCoy, Charles A. *Polk and the Presidency.* Austin: University of Texas Press, 1960.

Sellers, Charles G., Jr. *James K. Polk, Continentalist: 1843–1846.* Princeton, NJ: Princeton University Press, 1966.

————. *James K. Polk, Jacksonian: 1795–1843.* Princeton, NJ: Princeton University Press, 1957.

Zachary Taylor

Hamilton, Holman. *Zachary Taylor.* 2 vols. Indianapolis: Bobbs-Merrill, 1941–1951.

Smith, Elbert B. *The Presidencies of Zachary Taylor and Millard Fillmore.* Lawrence: University Press of Kansas, 1988.

Millard Fillmore

Rayback, Robert J. *Millard Fillmore: Biography of a President.* Buffalo, NY: Henry Stewart, 1959.

Smith, Elbert B. *The Presidencies of Zachary Taylor and Millard Fillmore.* Lawrence: University Press of Kansas, 1988.

Franklin Pierce

Gara, Larry. *The Presidency of Franklin Pierce.* Lawrence: University Press of Kansas, 1991.

Hoyt, Edwin P. *Franklin Pierce: The Fourteenth President of the United States.* New York: Harper and Row, 1972.

Nichols, Roy F. *Franklin Pierce: Young Hickory of the Granite Hills.* 2d ed. Philadelphia: University of Pennsylvania Press, 1969.

James Buchanan

Curtis, George T. *Life of James Buchanan, Fifteenth President of the United States.* 2 vols. New York: Harper, 1883.

Klein, Philip S. *President James Buchanan: A Biography.* University Park: Pennsylvania State University Press, 1962.

Smith, Elbert B. *The Presidency of James Buchanan.* Lawrence: University Press of Kansas, 1975.

Abraham Lincoln

Cox, LaWanda C. *Lincoln and Black Freedom: A Study in Presidential Leadership.* Urbana: University of Illinois Press, 1985.

Current, Richard N. *Speaking of Abraham Lincoln: The Man and His Meaning for Our Times.* Urbana: University of Illinois Press, 1983.

Fehrenbacher, Don E. *The Leadership of Abraham Lincoln.* New York: Wiley, 1970.

Findley, Paul A. *Lincoln, the Crucible of Congress.* New York: Crown, 1979.

Handlin, Oscar, and Lilian Handlin. *Abraham Lincoln and the Union.* Boston: Little, Brown, 1980.

Herndon, William H., and J. William Weik. *Herndon's Lincoln: The True Story of a Great Life, the History and Personal Recollections of Abraham Lincoln.* 3 vols. Chicago: Belford, Clarke, 1889.

Neely, Mark E. *The Fate of Liberty: Abraham Lincoln and Civil Liberties.* New York: Oxford University Press, 1991.

Nevins, Allan. *The Emergence of Lincoln.* 2 vols. New York: Scribner's 1950.

Oates, Stephen B. *Abraham Lincoln: The Man behind the Myths.* New York: Harper and Row, 1984.

Paludan, Phillip S. *The Presidency of Abraham Lincoln.* Lawrence: University Press of Kansas, 1994.

Sandburg, Carl. *Abraham Lincoln, The Prairie Years.* 2 vols. New York: Harcourt Brace, 1926.

————. *Abraham Lincoln: The War Years.* 4 vols. New York: Harcourt Brace, 1939.

Wills, Garry. *Lincoln at Gettysburg: The Words That Remade America.* New York: Simon and Schuster, 1992.

Andrew Johnson

Beale, Howard K. *The Critical Year: A Study of Andrew Johnson and the Reconstruction.* New York: Harcourt Brace, 1930.

Castel, Albert. *The Presidency of Andrew Johnson.* Lawrence: Regents Press of Kansas, 1979.

DeWitt, David M. *The Impeachment and Trial of Andrew Johnson, Seventeenth President of the United States: A History.* New York: Macmillan, 1903.

McKitrick, Eric L. *Andrew Johnson and Reconstruction.* Chicago: University of Chicago Press, 1960.

Sefton, James E. *Andrew Johnson and the Uses of Constitutional Power.* Boston: Little, Brown, 1980.

Trefousse, Hans L. *Andrew Johnson: A Biography.* New York: W. W. Norton, 1989.

Ulysses S. Grant

Carpenter, John A. *Ulysses S. Grant.* New York: Twayne, 1970.

Catton, Bruce. *U.S. Grant and the American Military Tradition.* Boston: Little, Brown, 1954.

Mantell, Martin E. *Johnson, Grant, and the Politics of Reconstruction.* New York: Columbia University Press, 1973.

McFeely, William S. *Grant, a Biography.* New York: W. W. Norton, 1981.

Simpson, Brooks D. *Let Us Have Peace: Ulysses S. Grant and the Politics of War and Reconstruction, 1861–1868.* Chapel Hill: University of North Carolina Press, 1991.

Woodward, William E. *Meet General Grant.* New York: Liveright, 1928.

Rutherford B. Hayes

Davison, Kenneth E. *The Presidency of Rutherford B. Hayes.* Westport, CT: Greenwood Press, 1972.

Hoogenboom, Ari A. *The Presidency of Rutherford B. Hayes.* Lawrence: University Press of Kansas, 1988.

Morgan, H. Wayne. *From Hayes to McKinley: National Party Politics, 1877–1896.* Syracuse, NY: Syracuse University Press, 1969.

James A. Garfield

Booraem, Hendrik. *The Road to Respectability: James A. Garfield and His World, 1844–1852.* Lewisburg, PA: Bucknell University Press; Cleveland: Western Reserve Historical Society Press, 1988.

Doenecke, Justus D. *The Presidencies of James A. Garfield and Chester A. Arthur.* Lawrence: Regents Press of Kansas, 1981.

Peskin, Allan. *Garfield: A Biography.* Kent, OH: Kent State University Press, 1978.

Chester A. Arthur

Doenecke, Justus D. *The Presidencies of James A. Garfield and Chester A. Arthur.* Lawrence: Regents Press of Kansas, 1981.

Reeves, Thomas C. *Gentleman Boss: The Life of Chester Alan Arthur.* New York: Knopf, 1975.

Grover Cleveland

McElroy, Robert M. *Grover Cleveland, The Man and the Statesman: An Authorized Biography.* 2 vols. New York: Harper and Row, 1923.

Merrill, Horace S. *Bourbon Leader: Grover Cleveland and the Democratic Party.* Boston: Little, Brown, 1957.

Nevins, Allan. *Grover Cleveland: A Study in Courage.* New York: Dodd, Mead, 1932.

Welch, Richard E. *The Presidencies of Grover Cleveland.* Lawrence: University Press of Kansas, 1988.

Benjamin Harrison

Sievers, Harry J. *Benjamin Harrison: Hoosier President: The White House and After.* New York: University Publishers, 1968.

———. *Benjamin Harrison: Hoosier Statesman from the Civil War to the White House: 1865–1888.* New York: University Publishers, 1959.

———. *Benjamin Harrison: Hoosier Warrior: 1833–1865, Through the Civil War Years.* 2d ed. New York: University Publishers, 1960.

William McKinley

Gould, Lewis L. *The Presidency of William McKinley.* Lawrence: Regents Press of Kansas, 1980.

Morgan, H. Wayne. *William McKinley and His America.* Syracuse, NY: Syracuse University Press, 1963.

Theodore Roosevelt

Blum, John M. *The Progressive Presidents: Roosevelt, Wilson, Roosevelt, Johnson.* New York: W. W. Norton, 1980.

———. *The Republican Roosevelt.* 2d ed. Cambridge, MA: Harvard University Press, 1977.

Burton, David. *The Learned Presidency: Theodore Roosevelt, William Howard Taft, Woodrow Wilson.* Rutherford, NJ: Fairleigh Dickinson University Press, 1988.

Cooper, John M., Jr. *The Warrior and the Priest: Theodore Roosevelt and Woodrow Wilson.* Cambridge, MA: Harvard University Press, 1983.

Gould, Lewis L. *The Presidency of Theodore Roosevelt.* Lawrence: University Press of Kansas, 1991.

Harbaugh, William H. *The Life and Times of Theodore Roosevelt.* Rev. ed. New York: Oxford University Press, 1975.

Miller, Nathan. *Theodore Roosevelt: A Life.* New York: William Morrow and Company, 1992.

Morris, Edmund. *The Rise of Theodore Roosevelt.* New York: Coward, McCann and Geoghegan, 1979.

Mowry, George E. *The Era of Theodore Roosevelt, 1900–1912.* New York: Harper and Row, 1958.

———. *Theodore Roosevelt and the Progressive Movement.* Madison: University of Wisconsin Press, 1946.

William Howard Taft

Anderson, Judith I. *William Howard Taft: An Intimate History.* New York: W. W. Norton, 1981.

Burton, David. *The Learned Presidency: Theodore Roosevelt, William Howard Taft, Woodrow Wilson.* Rutherford, NJ: Fairleigh Dickinson University Press, 1988.

Coletta, Paolo E. *The Presidency of William Howard Taft.* Lawrence: University Press of Kansas, 1973.

Mason, Alpheus T. *William Howard Taft: Chief Justice.* New York: Simon and Schuster, 1965.

Pringle, Henry F. *The Life and Times of William Howard Taft: A Biography.* 2 vols. New York: Farrar, Straus, 1939.

Woodrow Wilson

Baker, Ray S. *Woodrow Wilson: Life and Letters.* 8 vols. Garden City, NY: Doubleday, 1927–1939.

Blum, John M. *The Progressive Presidents: Roosevelt, Wilson, Roosevelt, Johnson.* New York: W. W. Norton, 1980.

Burton, David. *The Learned Presidency: Theodore Roosevelt, William Howard Taft, Woodrow Wilson.* Rutherford, NJ: Fairleigh Dickinson University Press, 1988.

Canfield, Leon H. *The Presidency of Woodrow Wilson: Prelude to a World in Crisis.* Rutherford, NJ: Fairleigh Dickinson University Press, 1966.

Clements, Kendrick A. *The Presidency of Woodrow Wilson.* Lawrence: University Press of Kansas, 1992.

Cooper, John M., Jr. *The Warrior and the Priest: Theodore Roosevelt and Woodrow Wilson.* Cambridge, MA: Belknap Press, 1983.

Knock, Thomas J. *To End All Wars: Woodrow Wilson and the Quest for a New World Order.* New York: Oxford University Press, 1992.

Link, Arthur S. *Wilson: Confusions and Crises: 1915–1916.* Princeton, NJ: Princeton University Press, 1964.

———. *Wilson: The Road to the White House.* Princeton, NJ: Princeton University Press, 1947.

———. *Wilson: The Struggle for Neutrality, 1914–1915.* Princeton, NJ: Princeton University Press, 1960.

———. *Woodrow Wilson.* 5 vols. Princeton, NJ: Princeton University Press, 1947–1965.

———. *Woodrow Wilson and a Revolutionary World, 1913–1921.* Chapel Hill: University of North Carolina Press, 1982.

———. *Woodrow Wilson and the Progressive Era, 1910–1917.* New York: Harper and Row, 1954.

Walworth, Arthur C. *Woodrow Wilson.* 3d ed. New York: W. W. Norton, 1978.

Warren G. Harding

Downes, Randolph C. *The Rise of Warren Gamaliel Harding: 1865–1920.* Columbus: Ohio State University Press, 1970.

Murray, Robert K. *The Harding Era: Warren G. Harding and His Administration*. Minneapolis: University of Minnesota Press, 1969.

————. *The Politics of Normalcy: Governmental Theory and Practice in the Harding–Coolidge Era*. New York: W. W. Norton, 1973.

Russell, Francis. *The Shadow of Blooming Grove: Warren G. Harding in His Times*. New York: McGraw-Hill, 1968.

Sinclair, Andrew. *The Available Man: The Life Behind the Masks of Warren Gamaliel Harding*. New York: Macmillan, 1965.

Trani, Eugene P., and David L. Wilson. *The Presidency of Warren G. Harding*. Lawrence: Regents Press of Kansas, 1977.

Calvin Coolidge

Fuess, Claude M. *Calvin Coolidge, The Man from Vermont*. Boston: Little, Brown, 1940.

McCoy, Donald R. *Calvin Coolidge, The Quiet President*. Lawrence: University Press of Kansas, 1988.

Murray, Robert K. *The Politics of Normalcy: Governmental Theory and Practice in the Harding-Coolidge Era*. New York: W. W. Norton, 1973.

Herbert Hoover

Best, Gary D. *Herbert Hoover: The Postpresidential Years, 1933–1964*. 2 vols. Stanford, CA: Hoover Institution Press, 1983.

————. *The Politics of American Individualism: Herbert Hoover in Transition, 1918–1921*. Westport, CT: Greenwood Press, 1975.

Burner, David. *Herbert Hoover: A Public Life*. New York: Knopf, 1979.

Fausold, Martin L. *The Presidency of Herbert Hoover*. Lawrence: University Press of Kansas, 1985.

Fausold, Martin L., and George Mazuzan, eds. *The Hoover Presidency: A Reappraisal*. Albany: State University of New York Press, 1974.

Hoff-Wilson, Joan. *Herbert Hoover, Forgotten Progressive*. Boston: Little, Brown, 1975.

Lisio, Donald J. *The Presidency and Protest: Hoover, Conspiracy, and the Bonus Riot.* Columbia: University of Missouri Press, 1974.

Nash, George H. *The Life of Herbert Hoover: The Engineer, 1874–1914.* New York: W. W. Norton, 1983.

————. *The Life of Herbert Hoover: The Humanitarian, 1914–1917.* New York: Norton, 1988.

Schwarz, Jordan A. *The Interregnum of Despair: Hoover, Congress, and the Depression.* Urbana: University of Illinois Press, 1970.

Smith, Richard N. *An Uncommon Man: The Triumph of Herbert Hoover.* New York: Simon and Schuster, 1984.

Warren, Harris G. *Herbert Hoover and the Great Depression.* New York: Oxford University Press, 1959.

Franklin D. Roosevelt

Abbott, Philip. *The Exemplary Presidency: Franklin D. Roosevelt and the American Political Tradition.* Amherst: University of Massachusetts Press, 1990.

Blum, John M. *The Progressive Presidents: Roosevelt, Wilson, Roosevelt, Johnson.* New York: W. W. Norton, 1980.

Burns, James M. *Roosevelt: The Lion and the Fox.* New York: Harcourt Brace, 1956.

————. *Roosevelt: The Soldier of Freedom.* New York: Harcourt Brace, 1970.

Dallek, Robert. *Franklin D. Roosevelt and American Foreign Policy, 1932–1945.* New York: Oxford University Press, 1979.

Davis, Kenneth S. *FDR, into the Storm 1937–1940: A History.* New York: Random House, 1993.

Freidel, Frank B. *Franklin D. Roosevelt.* 4 vols. Boston: Little, Brown, 1952–1973.

————. *Franklin D. Roosevelt: A Rendezvous with Destiny.* Boston: Little, Brown, 1990.

Leuchtenburg, William E. *Franklin D. Roosevelt and the New Deal, 1932–1940.* New York: Harper and Row, 1963.

Miller, Nathan. *FDR: An Intimate History.* Garden City, NY: Doubleday, 1983.

Morgan, Ted. *FDR.* New York: Simon and Schuster, 1985.

Nevins, Allan. *The Place of Franklin D. Roosevelt in History.* New York: Humanities Press, 1965.

Schlesinger, Arthur M., Jr. *The Age of Roosevelt.* 3 vols. Boston: Houghton Mifflin, 1957–1960.

Tugwell, Rexford G. *F.D.R.: The Architect of an Era.* New York: Macmillan, 1967.

Ward, Geoffrey C. *Before the Trumpet: Young Franklin Roosevelt 1882–1905.* New York: Harper and Row, 1985.

———. *A First Class Temperament: The Emergence of Franklin Roosevelt.* New York: Harper and Row, 1989.

Harry S. Truman

Daniels, Jonathan. *The Man of Independence.* Philadelphia: Lippincott, 1950.

Donovan, Robert J. *Conflict and Crisis: Presidency of Harry S. Truman: 1945–1948.* New York: W. W. Norton, 1977.

———. *Tumultuous Years: The Presidency of Harry S. Truman, 1949–1953.* New York: W. W. Norton, 1982.

Ferrell, Robert H. *Harry S. Truman: A Life.* Columbia: University of Missouri Press, 1994.

———. *Harry S. Truman and the Modern American Presidency.* Boston: Little, Brown, 1983.

Lacey, Michael J., ed. *The Truman Presidency.* New York: Cambridge University Press, 1989.

McCoy, Donald R. *The Presidency of Harry S. Truman.* Lawrence: University Press of Kansas, 1984.

McCullough, David G. *Truman*. New York: Simon and Schuster, 1992.

Dwight D. Eisenhower

Alexander, Charles C. *Holding the Line: The Eisenhower Era, 1952–1961*. Bloomington: Indiana University Press, 1975.

Ambrose, Stephen E. *Eisenhower: President and Elder Statesman, 1952–1969*. New York: Simon and Schuster, 1984.

————. *Eisenhower: Soldier and President*. New York: Simon and Schuster, 1990.

————. *Eisenhower: Soldier, General of the Army, President-Elect*. New York: Simon and Schuster, 1983.

————. *Ike: Abilene to Berlin*. New York: Harper and Row, 1973.

————. *The Supreme Commander: The War Years of General Dwight D. Eisenhower*. Garden City, NY: Doubleday, 1970.

Greenstein, Fred I. *The Hidden Hand Presidency: Eisenhower as Leader*. New York: Basic Books, 1982.

Pach, Chester J. *The Presidency of Dwight D. Eisenhower*. Lawrence: University Press of Kansas, 1991.

Parmet, Herbert S. *Eisenhower and the American Crusades*. New York: Macmillan, 1972.

John F. Kennedy

Beschloss, Michael R. *The Crisis Years: Kennedy and Khrushchev, 1960–1963*. New York: Edward Burlingame Books, 1991.

Giglio, James N. *The Presidency of John F. Kennedy*. Lawrence: University Press of Kansas, 1991.

Hamilton, Nigel. *JFK, Reckless Youth*. New York: Random House, 1992.

Miroff, Bruce. *Pragmatic Illusions: The Presidential Politics of John F. Kennedy*. New York: McKay, 1976.

Parmet, Herbert S. *Jack: The Struggles of John F. Kennedy.* New York: Dial, 1980.

———. *JFK: The Presidency of John F. Kennedy.* New York: Dial, 1983.

Reeves, Richard. *President Kennedy: Profile of Power.* New York: Simon and Schuster, 1993.

Schlesinger, Arthur M., Jr. *A Thousand Days: John F. Kennedy in the White House.* Boston: Houghton Mifflin, 1965.

Sorensen, Theodore C. *Kennedy.* New York: Harper and Row, 1965.

Wills, Garry. *The Kennedy Imprisonment: A Meditation on Power.* Boston: Little, Brown, 1982.

Lyndon B. Johnson

Blum, John M. *The Progressive Presidents: Roosevelt, Wilson, Roosevelt, Johnson.* New York: W. W. Norton, 1980.

Bornet, Vaughn D. *Presidency of Lyndon B. Johnson.* Lawrence: University Press of Kansas, 1983.

Califano, Joseph A. *The Triumph & Tragedy of Lyndon Johnson: The White House Years.* New York: Simon and Schuster, 1991.

Caro, Robert A. *Means of Ascent.* New York: Knopf, 1990.

———. *The Years of Lyndon Johnson: The Path to Power.* New York: Knopf, 1982.

Dallek, Robert. *Lone Star Rising: Lyndon Johnson and His Times, 1908–1960.* New York: Oxford University Press, 1991.

Dugger, Ronnie. *The Politician: The Life and Times of Lyndon Johnson: The Drive for Power, from the Frontier to Master of the Senate.* New York: W. W. Norton, 1982.

Goldman, Eric F. *The Tragedy of Lyndon Johnson: A Historian's Interpretation.* New York: Knopf, 1969.

Kearns, Doris. *Lyndon Johnson and the American Dream*. New York: Harper and Row, 1976.

Welborn, David M. *Regulation in the White House: The Johnson Presidency*. Austin: University of Texas Press, 1993.

Richard M. Nixon

Ambrose, Stephen E. *Nixon*. New York: Simon and Schuster, 1987–1991.

Brodie, Fawn M. *Richard Nixon: The Shaping of His Character*. Cambridge, MA: Harvard University Press, 1983.

Evans, Rowland, Jr., and Robert D. Novak. *Nixon in the White House: The Frustration of Power*. New York: Vintage, 1971.

Genovese, Michael A. *The Nixon Presidency: Power and Politics in Turbulent Times*. New York: Greenwood Press, 1990.

Hersh, Seymour M. *The Price of Power: Kissinger in the Nixon White House*. New York: Summit Books, 1983.

Hoff-Wilson, Joan. *Nixon Reconsidered*. New York: Basic Books, 1994.

Litwak, Robert S. *Detente and the Nixon Doctrine: American Foreign Policy and the Pursuit of Stability, 1969–1976*. New York: Cambridge University Press, 1984.

Morris, Roger. *Richard Milhous Nixon: The Rise of an American Politician*. New York: Holt, 1990.

Parmet, Herbert S. *Richard Nixon and His America*. Boston: Little, Brown, 1990.

Safire, William. *Before the Fall: An Inside View of the Pre-Watergate White House*. Garden City, NY: Doubleday, 1975.

Wicker, Tom. *One of Us: Richard Nixon and the American Dream*. New York: Random House, 1991.

Gerald R. Ford

Cannon, James M. *Time and Chance: Gerald Ford's Appointment with History*. New York: HarperCollins, 1994.

Greene, John R. *Gerald R. Ford: A Bibliography*. New York: Greenwood Press, 1994.

————. *The Presidency of Gerald R. Ford*. Lawrence: University Press of Kansas, 1995.

Reeves, Richard. *A Ford, Not a Lincoln*. New York: Harcourt Brace Jovanovich, 1975.

TerHorst, Jerald F. *Gerald Ford and the Future of the Presidency*. New York: Third Press, 1974.

Jimmy Carter

Campbell, Colin. *Managing the Presidency: Carter, Reagan, and the Search for Executive Harmony*. Pittsburgh: University of Pittsburgh Press, 1986.

Fink, Gary M. *Prelude to the Presidency: The Political Character and Legislative Leadership–Style of Governor Jimmy Carter*. Westport, CT: Greenwood Press, 1980.

Hargrove, Erwin C. *Jimmy Carter as President: Leadership and the Politics of the Public Good*. Baton Rouge: Louisiana State University Press, 1988.

Jones, Charles O. *The Trusteeship Presidency: Jimmy Carter and the United States Congress*. Baton Rouge: Louisiana State University Press, 1988.

Kaufman, Burton Ira. *The Presidency of James Earl Carter, Jr.* Lawrence: University Press of Kansas, 1993.

Lynn, Laurence E., Jr. *The President as Policy Maker: Jimmy Carter and Welfare Reform*. Philadelphia: Temple University Press, 1981.

Ronald Reagan

Campbell, Colin. *Managing the Presidency: Carter, Reagan, and the Search for Executive Harmony*. Pittsburgh: University of Pittsburgh Press, 1986.

Cannon, Lou. *President Reagan: The Role of a Lifetime*. New York: Simon and Schuster, 1991.

Dallek, Robert. *Ronald Reagan: The Politics of Symbolism*. Cambridge, MA: Harvard University Press, 1984.

Greenstein, Fred I. *The Reagan Presidency: An Early Assessment.* Baltimore: Johns Hopkins University Press, 1983.

George Bush

Campbell, Colin, and Bert A. Rockman, eds. *The Bush Presidency: First Appraisals.* Chatham, NJ: Chatham House, 1991.

Duffy, Michael. *Marching in Place: The Status Quo Presidency of George Bush.* New York: Simon and Schuster, 1992.

Hill, Dilys M., and Phil Williams, eds. *The Bush Presidency: Triumphs and Adversities.* New York: St. Martin's Press, 1994.

Kolb, Charles. *White House Daze: The Unmaking of Domestic Policy in the Bush Years.* New York: Free Press, 1994.

Bill Clinton

Cohen, Richard E. *Changing Course in Washington: Clinton and the New Congress.* New York: Macmillan, 1994.

Drew, Elizabeth. *On the Edge: The Clinton Presidency.* New York: Simon and Shuster, 1994.

Hohenberg, John. *The Bill Clinton Story: Winning the Presidency.* Syracuse, NY: Syracuse University Press, 1994.

Maraniss, David. *First in His Class: A Biography of Bill Clinton.* New York: Simon and Schuster, 1995.

Oakley, Meredith L. *On the Make: The Rise of Bill Clinton.* Washington, DC: Regnery, 1994.

Renshon, Stanley A., ed. *The Clinton Presidency: Campaigning, Governing, and the Psychology of Leadership.* Boulder, CO: Westview Press, 1994.

Woodward, Bob. *The Agenda: Inside the Clinton White House.* New York: Simon and Schuster, 1994.

Appendix

U.S. Presidents and Vice Presidents   114

Backgrounds of U.S. Presidents   116

Glossary   120

Appendix A.   U.S. Presidents and Vice Presidents

President and political party	Born	Died	Age at inauguration	Native of	Elected from	Term of service	Vice president
George Washington (F)	1732	1799	57	Va.	Va.	April 30, 1789–March 4, 1793	John Adams
George Washington (F)			61			March 4, 1793–March 4, 1797	John Adams
John Adams (F)	1735	1826	61	Mass.	Mass.	March 4, 1797–March 4, 1801	Thomas Jefferson
Thomas Jefferson (DR)	1743	1826	57	Va.	Va.	March 4, 1801–March 4, 1805	Aaron Burr
Thomas Jefferson (DR)			61			March 4, 1805–March 4, 1809	George Clinton
James Madison (DR)	1751	1836	57	Va.	Va.	March 4, 1809–March 4, 1813	George Clinton
James Madison (DR)			61			March 4, 1813–March 4, 1817	Elbridge Gerry
James Monroe (DR)	1758	1831	58	Va.	Va.	March 4, 1817–March 4, 1821	Daniel D. Tompkins
James Monroe (DR)			62			March 4, 1821–March 4, 1825	Daniel D. Tompkins
John Q. Adams (DR)	1767	1848	57	Mass.	Mass.	March 4, 1825–March 4, 1829	John C. Calhoun
Andrew Jackson (D)	1767	1845	61	S.C.	Tenn.	March 4, 1829–March 4, 1833	John C. Calhoun
Andrew Jackson (D)			65			March 4, 1833–March 4, 1837	Martin Van Buren
Martin Van Buren (D)	1782	1862	54	N.Y.	N.Y.	March 4, 1837–March 4, 1841	Richard M. Johnson
W. H. Harrison (W)	1773	1841	68	Va.	Ohio	March 4, 1841–April 4, 1841	John Tyler
John Tyler (W)	1790	1862	51	Va.	Va.	April 6, 1841–March 4, 1845	
James K. Polk (D)	1795	1849	49	N.C.	Tenn.	March 4, 1845–March 4, 1849	George M. Dallas
Zachary Taylor (W)	1784	1850	64	Va.	La.	March 4, 1849–July 9, 1850	Millard Fillmore
Millard Fillmore (W)	1800	1874	50	N.Y.	N.Y.	July 10, 1850–March 4, 1853	
Franklin Pierce (D)	1804	1869	48	N.H.	N.H.	March 4, 1853–March 4, 1857	William R. King
James Buchanan (D)	1791	1868	65	Pa.	Pa.	March 4, 1857–March 4, 1861	John C. Breckinridge
Abraham Lincoln (R)	1809	1865	52	Ky.	Ill.	March 4, 1861–March 4, 1865	Hannibal Hamlin
Abraham Lincoln (R)			56			March 4, 1865–April 15, 1865	Andrew Johnson
Andrew Johnson (R)	1808	1875	56	N.C.	Tenn.	April 15, 1865–March 4, 1869	
Ulysses S. Grant (R)	1822	1885	46	Ohio	Ill.	March 4, 1869–March 4, 1873	Schuyler Colfax
Ulysses S. Grant (R)			50			March 4, 1873–March 4, 1877	Henry Wilson
Rutherford B. Hayes (R)	1822	1893	54	Ohio	Ohio	March 4, 1877–March 4, 1881	William A. Wheeler
James A. Garfield (R)	1831	1881	49	Ohio	Ohio	March 4, 1881–Sept. 19, 1881	Chester A. Arthur
Chester A. Arthur (R)	1830	1886	50	Vt.	N.Y.	Sept. 20, 1881–March 4, 1885	
Grover Cleveland (D)	1837	1908	47	N.J.	N.Y.	March 4, 1885–March 4, 1889	Thomas A. Hendricks

	Born	Died	Age			Term	Vice President
Benjamin Harrison (R)	1833	1901	55	Ohio	Ind.	March 4, 1889–March 4, 1893	Levi P. Morton
Grover Cleveland (D)	1837	1908	55	N.J.	N.Y.	March 4, 1893–March 4, 1897	Adlai E. Stevenson
William McKinley (R)	1843	1901	54	Ohio	Ohio	March 4, 1897–March 4, 1901	Garret A. Hobart
William McKinley (R)			58			March 4, 1901–Sept. 14, 1901	Theodore Roosevelt
Theodore Roosevelt (R)	1858	1919	42	N.Y.	N.Y.	Sept. 14, 1901–March 4, 1905	
Theodore Roosevelt (R)			46			March 4, 1905–March 4, 1909	Charles W. Fairbanks
William H. Taft (R)	1857	1930	51	Ohio	Ohio	March 4, 1909–March 4, 1913	James S. Sherman
Woodrow Wilson (D)	1856	1924	56	Va.	N.J.	March 4, 1913–March 4, 1917	Thomas R. Marshall
Woodrow Wilson (D)			60			March 4, 1917–March 4, 1921	Thomas R. Marshall
Warren G. Harding (R)	1865	1923	55	Ohio	Ohio	March 4, 1921–Aug. 2, 1923	Calvin Coolidge
Calvin Coolidge (R)	1872	1933	51	Vt.	Mass.	Aug. 3, 1923–March 4, 1925	
Calvin Coolidge (R)			52			March 4, 1925–March 4, 1929	Charles G. Dawes
Herbert Hoover (R)	1874	1964	54	Iowa	Calif.	March 4, 1929–March 4, 1933	Charles Curtis
Franklin D. Roosevelt (D)	1882	1945	51	N.Y.	N.Y.	March 4, 1933–Jan. 20, 1937	John N. Garner
Franklin D. Roosevelt (D)			55			Jan. 20, 1937–Jan. 20, 1941	John N. Garner
Franklin D. Roosevelt (D)			59			Jan. 20, 1941–Jan. 20, 1945	Henry A. Wallace
Franklin D. Roosevelt (D)			63			Jan. 20, 1945–April 12, 1945	Harry S. Truman
Harry S. Truman (D)	1884	1972	60	Mo.	Mo.	April 12, 1945–Jan. 20, 1949	
Harry S. Truman (D)			64			Jan. 20, 1949–Jan. 20, 1953	Alben W. Barkley
Dwight D. Eisenhower (R)	1890	1969	62	Texas	N.Y.	Jan. 20, 1953–Jan. 20, 1957	Richard Nixon
Dwight D. Eisenhower (R)			66		Pa.	Jan. 20, 1957–Jan. 20, 1961	Richard Nixon
John F. Kennedy (D)	1917	1963	43	Mass.	Mass.	Jan. 20, 1961–Nov. 22, 1963	Lyndon B. Johnson
Lyndon B. Johnson (D)	1908	1973	55	Texas	Texas	Nov. 22, 1963–Jan. 20, 1965	
Lyndon B. Johnson (D)			56			Jan. 20, 1965–Jan. 20, 1969	Hubert H. Humphrey
Richard Nixon (R)	1913	1994	56	Calif.	N.Y.	Jan. 20, 1969–Jan. 20, 1973	Spiro T. Agnew
Richard Nixon (R)			60		Calif.	Jan. 20, 1973–Aug. 9, 1974	Spiro T. Agnew; Gerald R. Ford
Gerald R. Ford (R)	1913		61	Neb.	Mich.	Aug. 9, 1974–Jan. 20, 1977	Nelson A. Rockefeller
Jimmy Carter (D)	1924		52	Ga.	Ga.	Jan. 20, 1977–Jan. 20, 1981	Walter F. Mondale
Ronald Reagan (R)	1911		69	Ill.	Calif.	Jan. 20, 1981–Jan. 20, 1985	George Bush
Ronald Reagan (R)			73			Jan. 20, 1985–Jan. 20, 1989	George Bush
George Bush (R)	1924		64	Mass.	Texas	Jan. 20, 1989–Jan. 20, 1993	Dan Quayle
Bill Clinton (D)	1946		46	Ark.	Ark.	Jan. 20, 1993–	Albert Gore, Jr.

Source: *Presidential Elections Since 1789*, 4th ed. (Washington, DC: Congressional Quarterly, 1987), 4.

Note: D—Democrat; DR—Democratic-Republican; F—Federalist; R—Republican; W—Whig.

Appendix B.   Backgrounds of U.S. Presidents

President	Age at first political office	First political office	Last political office[a]	Age at becoming president	State of residence[b]	Father's occupation	Higher education[c]	Occupation
1. Washington (1789–1797)	17	County surveyor	Commander in chief	57	Va.	Farmer	None	Farmer, surveyor
2. Adams, J. (1797–1801)	39	Surveyor of highways	Vice president	61	Mass.	Farmer	Harvard	Farmer, lawyer
3. Jefferson (1801–1809)	26	State legislator	Vice president	58	Va.	Farmer	William and Mary	Farmer, lawyer
4. Madison (1809–1817)	25	State legislator	Secretary of state	58	Va.	Farmer	Princeton	Farmer
5. Monroe (1817–1825)	24	State legislator	Secretary of state	59	Va.	Farmer	William and Mary	Lawyer, farmer
6. Adams, J. Q. (1825–1829)	27	Minister to Netherlands	Secretary of state	58	Mass.	Farmer, lawyer	Harvard	Lawyer
7. Jackson (1829–1837)	21	Prosecuting attorney	U.S. Senate	62	Tenn.	Farmer	None	Lawyer
8. Van Buren (1837–1841)	30	Surrogate of county	Vice president	55	N.Y.	Tavern keeper	None	Lawyer
9. Harrison, W. H. (1841)	26	Territorial delegate to Congress	Minister to Colombia	68	Ind.	Farmer	Hampden–Sydney	Military
10. Tyler (1841–1845)	21	State legislator	Vice president	51	Va.	Planter, lawyer	William and Mary	Lawyer

President	Age	First office	Highest prior office	Age	State	Father's occupation	College	Occupation
11. Polk (1845–1849)	28	State legislator	Governor	50	Tenn.	Surveyor	U. of North Carolina	Lawyer
12. Taylor (1849–1850)	—	None	a	65	Ky.	Collector of internal revenue	None	Military
13. Fillmore (1850–1853)	28	State legislator	Vice president	50	N.Y.	Farmer	None	Lawyer
14. Pierce (1853–1857)	25	State legislator	U.S. district attorney	48	N.H.	General	Bowdoin	Lawyer
15. Buchanan (1857–1861)	22	Assistant county prosecutor	Minister to Great Britain	65	Pa.	Farmer	Dickinson	Lawyer
16. Lincoln (1861–1865)	25	State legislator	U.S. House of Representatives	52	Ill.	Farmer, carpenter	None	Lawyer
17. Johnson, A. (1865–1869)	20	City alderman	Vice president	57	Tenn.	Janitor–porter	None	Tailor
18. Grant (1869–1877)	—	None	a	47	Ohio	Tanner	West Point	Military
19. Hayes (1877–1881)	36	City solicitor	Governor	55	Ohio	Farmer	Kenyon	Lawyer
20. Garfield (1881)	28	State legislator	U.S. Senate	50	Ohio	Canal worker	Williams	Educator, lawyer
21. Arthur (1881–1885)	31	State engineer	Vice president	51	N.Y.	Minister	Union	Lawyer
22. Cleveland (1885–1889) 24. (1893–1897)	26	Assistant district attorney	Governor	48	N.Y.	Minister	None	Lawyer
23. Harrison, B. (1889–1893)	24	City attorney	U.S. Senate	56	Ind.	Military	Miami of Ohio	Lawyer
25. McKinley (1897–1901)	26	Prosecuting attorney	Governor	54	Ohio	Ironmonger	Allegheny	Lawyer

President	Age at first political office	First political office	Last political office[a]	Age at becoming president	State of residence[b]	Father's occupation	Higher education[c]	Occupation
26. Roosevelt, T. (1901–1909)	24	State legislator	Vice president	43	N.Y.	Businessman	Harvard	Lawyer, author
27. Taft (1909–1913)	24	Assistant prose-cuting attorney	Secretary of war	52	Ohio	Lawyer	Yale	Lawyer
28. Wilson (1913–1921)	54	Governor	Governor	56	N.J.	Minister	Princeton	Educator
29. Harding (1921–1923)	35	State legislator	U.S. Senate	56	Ohio	Physician, editor	Ohio Central	Newspaper editor
30. Coolidge (1923–1929)	26	City councilman	Vice president	51	Mass.	Storekeeper	Amherst	Lawyer
31. Hoover (1929–1933)	43	Relief and food administrator	Secretary of commerce	55	Calif.	Blacksmith	Stanford	Mining engineer
32. Roosevelt, F. (1933–1945)	28	State legislator	Governor	49	N.Y.	Businessman, landowner	Harvard	Lawyer
33. Truman (1945–1953)	38	County judge (commissioner)	Vice president	61	Mo.	Farmer, livestock	None	Clerk, store owner
34. Eisenhower (1953–1961)	—	None	[a]	63	Kan.	Mechanic	West Point	Military
35. Kennedy (1961–1963)	29	U.S. House of Representatives	U.S. Senate	43	Mass.	Businessman	Harvard	Newspaper reporter
36. Johnson, L. (1963–1969)	23	Assistant to mem-ber, U.S. House of Representatives	Vice president	55	Texas	Farmer, real estate	Southwest Texas State Teacher's College	Educator

President	Age	Last civilian office[a]	Office	Age	Father's occupation	College[c]	Occupation
37. Nixon (1969–1974)	29	Office of Price Administration	Vice president	56	Streetcar conductor	Whittier	Lawyer
38. Ford (1974–1977)	36	U.S. House of Representatives	Vice president	61	Businessman	U. of Michigan	Lawyer
39. Carter (1977–1981)	38	County Board of Education	Governor	52	Farmer, businessman	U.S. Naval Academy	Farmer, businessman
40. Reagan (1981–1989)	55	Governor	Governor	69	Shoe salesman	Eureka	Entertainer
41. Bush (1989–1993)	42	U.S. House of Representatives	Vice president	64	Businessman, U.S. senator	Yale	Businessman
42. Clinton (1993–)	30	State attorney general	Governor	46	Salesman	Georgetown	Lawyer

Source: Richard A. Watson and Norman C. Thomas, *The Politics of the Presidency,* 2d ed. (Washington, DC: CQ Press, 1988), 515–519.

[a] This category refers to the last civilian office held before the presidency. Taylor, Grant, and Eisenhower had served as generals before becoming president.

[b] The state is where the president spent his important adult years, not necessarily where he was born.

[c] Refers to undergraduate education.

Glossary

Act. Legislation that has become law after having cleared both houses of Congress and been signed by the president or cleared over the presidential veto.

Appointment and Removal Power. The power of the president to select and dismiss top officials in the executive branch. In order for an administration to function smoothly, it is essential that the president make sure executive officials are competent, qualified, trustworthy, and in agreement with the president. Appointees must be confirmed by the Senate.

Chief of Staff. The most important member of the White House staff. This person functions as a manager, adviser, and traffic controller. The chief of staff also can cover unpleasant jobs like reprimanding or dismissing members of the administration and accepting the responsibility for errors made by the president.

Commissions, Presidential. Groups selected by the president to research specific topics that are beyond the daily scope of presidential advisory organizations in order to aid in decision making. There are three types of presidential commissions: permanent federal advisory organizations, ad hoc or "blue ribbon" commissions (which can last a maximum of three years), and White House conferences (which generally last a few days).

Diplomatic Powers. The control the Constitution grants the president to be used in foreign affairs. In general, the president possesses the most power over foreign affairs, while Congress serves to balance and check the president. The president commands the armed forces, but only Congress can declare war; the president makes treaties, but not without the advice and consent of the Senate; the president appoints ambassadors, but the Senate must confirm them.

Disability Amendment. The Twenty-fifth Amendment, which was adopted in 1967 to determine what should be done if a president becomes disabled. The first part of the amendment is applicable to presidents who admit they are unable to fulfill their duties. In this case, the president must write a letter to the Speaker of the House and to the president pro tempore of the Senate, giving presidential power to the vice president. The second part applies to the case wherein the president is unable or unwilling to admit to being disabled. In this case, the vice president and a majority of the heads of the executive departments may declare the vice president to be acting president. In both cases, the president's power would be restored by a letter from the president declaring the end of the disability.

Economic Advisers, Council of. A three-member body, appointed by the president and confirmed by the Senate, which serves to provide the president with expert nonpartisan economic advice. The Council of Economic Advisers (CEA) prepares the president's annual economic report.

Economic Powers. The economic responsibilities of the president. The Constitution does not grant the president specific economic powers— rather, it gives the president the duty of acting as an overseer, leader, foreign negotiator, and manager of economic policy and decisions made by Congress.

Electoral College. A group of electors who elect the president. Each state is allocated as many electors as it has representatives and senators in Congress. Citizens vote indirectly for the president by voting for these electors. For the most part, the electoral college chooses the candidate who wins the popular vote, but this is not always the case. If no candidate wins the majority of the electoral votes, the House of Representatives chooses the president.

Emergency Powers. Extraordinary powers the president may use in urgent times to preserve the nation, to promote the general welfare, or to provide for the common good of the people. Times at which the president might use emergency powers are during war, economic crises, domestic unrest, and natural disasters.

Executive Agreement. A pact other than a treaty made by the president or representatives of the president with a foreign leader or government. The president can make executive agreements without obtaining the two-thirds majority of the Senate required to ratify a treaty. Executive agreements are binding and have the force of law, but, unlike treaties, they do not supersede U.S. laws with which they conflict.

Executive Calendar. This is a nonlegislative calendar in the Senate on which presidential documents such as treaties and nominations are listed.

Executive Document. A document, usually a treaty, sent to the Senate by the president for consideration. Such documents are referred to committee in the same manner as other measures. Unlike legislative documents, however, treaties do not die at the end of a congress but remain alive until they are either acted on by the Senate or withdrawn by the president.

Executive Office of the President. A collection of agencies who help the president oversee department and agency activities, formulate budgets and monitor spending, craft legislation, and lobby Congress. The heads of the Executive Office of the President (EOP) are appointed by the president and approved by the Senate.

Executive Orders. Presidential proclamations that carry the force of law. Executive orders may be used to enforce the Constitution or treaties with foreign countries, help execute laws, direct bureaucratic agencies, or protect and promote the civil rights of all Americans.

Executive Privilege. The limited right of the president to withhold sensitive information from Congress or the courts.

Executive Veto. Disapproval by the president of a bill or joint resolution (other than one proposing an amendment to the Constitution). When Congress is in session, the president must veto a bill within ten days, excluding Sundays, after he has received it; otherwise, it becomes law without his signature. When the president vetoes a bill, he returns it to the house of origin along with a message stating his objections.

Impeachment. The power given to Congress by the Constitution to remove a president from office. This power gives Congress the ultimate check on executive and judicial authority. The House of Representatives is the prosecutor in impeachment proceedings; the Senate, with the chief justice of the Supreme Court presiding, is the judge and jury.

Item Veto. The controversial power of the president to veto certain parts or items of a bill, without vetoing the entire bill, also known as line-item veto. This is a veto power which many have argued for and against.

Law. An act of Congress that has been signed by the president or been passed over a presidential veto by Congress. Public bills, when signed, become public laws, and are cited by the letters "PL" and a hyphenated number. The number preceding the hyphen corresponds to the congress, while the one or more digits after the hyphen refer to the numerical sequence in which the president signed the bill during that congress. Private bills, when signed, become private laws.

Legislative Veto. A procedure that permitted the House or Senate to review proposed executive branch regulations or actions and to block or modify those with which they disagreed. Congress generally provided for a legislative veto by including in a bill a provision that administrative rules or action taken to implement the law were to go into effect at the end of a designated period of time unless blocked by either or both houses of Congress. Another version of the veto provided for congressional reconsideration and rejection of regulations already in effect. The Supreme Court in 1983 struck down the legislative veto as an unconstitutional violation of the lawmaking procedure provided in the Constitution.

Lobby. A group seeking to influence the passage or defeat of legislation. Originally the term referred to persons frequenting the lobbies or corridors of legislative chambers to speak to lawmakers. The definition of a lobby and the activity of lobbying is a matter of differing interpretation. By some definitions, lobbying is limited to direct attempts to influence lawmakers through personal interviews and persuasion. Under other definitions, lobbying includes attempts at indirect, or "grass-roots," influence, such as persuading members of a group to write or visit their district's representative and state's senators or attempting to create a climate of opinion favorable to a desired legislative goal. The right to attempt to influence legislation is based on the First Amendment to the Constitution, which says Congress shall make no law abridging the right of the people "to petition the government for a redress of grievances."

Management and Budget, Office of. The agency which analyzes the merits of budget requests and recommends to the president what funding should be cut, preserved, or expanded. The Office of Management and Budget (OMB) brings together the president's national budget plan.

National Security Adviser. The person who oversees the functions of the National Security Council (NSC) staff and performs whatever foreign policy duties the president designates. This adviser is not confirmed by the Senate and does not possess legal authority like a cabinet member. The extent of the adviser's power is completely up to the president.

National Security Council. A presidential advisory body consisting of the president, vice president, and secretaries of defense and state which coordinates the actions of government agencies into a coherent foreign policy. The National Security Council (NSC) was created in 1947 by the National Security Act.

Nominations. Presidential appointments to office subject to Senate confirmation. Although most nominations win quick Senate approval, some are controversial and become the topic of hearings and debate. Sometimes senators object to appointees for patronage reasons, for example, when a nomination to a local federal job is made without consulting the senators of the state concerned. In some situations a senator may object that the nominee is "personally obnoxious." Usually other senators join in blocking such appointments out of courtesy to their colleagues.

Override a Veto. If the president disapproves a bill and sends it back to Congress with objections, Congress may try to override the veto and enact the bill into law. The override of a veto requires a recorded vote with a two-thirds majority of those present and voting in each chamber. Neither house is required to attempt an override.

Pocket Veto. The act of the president in withholding his approval of a bill after Congress has adjourned. When Congress is in session, a bill becomes law without the president's signature if he does not act upon it within ten days, excluding Sundays, from the time he gets it. But if Congress adjourns sine die within that ten day period, the bill will die even if the president does not formally veto it.

Press Conference. An impromptu meeting called by the president in which reporters ask the president questions.

Qualifications of the President. The requirements for being eligible to be the president of the United States. To be president, one must be a native-born United States citizen, be over thirty-five years old, and have lived in the United States for the last fourteen years.

Separation of Powers. The constitutional idea that the three branches of the government must remain separate, especially in terms of membership and also in terms of authority, in order to maintain a system of checks and balances.

State of the Union Address. A report given by the president every year in front of a joint session of Congress, the Supreme Court, and cabinet members which outlines the state of the nation.

Statutes at Large. A chronological arrangement of the laws enacted in each session of Congress. Though indexed, the statutes are not arranged by subject matter, and there is no indication of how they may have changed previously enacted laws.

Succession. The replacement of the president by the vice president or whoever is next in line in the event of the president dying, becoming disabled, or being removed from office. As of 1947 the line of succession has been: vice president, Speaker of the House, president pro tempore of the Senate, secretary of state, secretary of the treasury, secretary of defense, attorney general, and, in order, the secretaries of interior, agriculture, commerce, labor, health and human services, housing and urban development, transportation, energy, education, and veterans affairs.

Term of Office. The time limit a president is allowed to hold office. Each term lasts four years and presidents are limited to being elected twice. If a successor president has served more than two years of a departed president's four-year term, the successor may only be elected once.

Treaties. Executive proposals in the form of resolutions of ratification that must be submitted to the Senate for approval by two-thirds of the members present. Treaties are normally sent to the Foreign Relations Committee for scrutiny before the Senate takes action. Foreign Relations has jurisdiction over all treaties, regardless of subject matter. Treaties are read three times and debated on the floor in much the same manner as legislative proposals. After Senate approval, treaties are formally ratified by the president.

U.S. Code. A consolidation and codification of the general and permanent laws of the United States arranged by subject under fifty titles, the first six dealing with general or political subjects, and the other forty-four alphabetically arranged from agriculture to war. The U.S. Code is updated annually, and a new set of bound volumes is published every six years.

Veto. Executive disapproval of a bill or joint resolution, other than one that proposes an amendment to the Constitution. When Congress is in session, the president must veto a bill within ten days excluding Sundays of its receipt; otherwise, the bill becomes law without his signature. When the president vetoes a bill, he returns it to the house of origin along with a message stating his objections.

War Powers. The power to use the military against foreign nations. The Constitution splits the war powers among the legislative and executive branches to prevent tyranny. Only Congress can declare war, but the president is the commander in chief of the military and is allowed to make speedy military decisions in emergency cases. The president possesses the power to authorize the use of nuclear weapons for defense without first obtaining congressional permission.

Author Index

Ali, Sheikh R., 8
Androit, John, 37
Anzovin, Steven, 35
Aristotle Political Campaign Videos,
49

Bevans, Charles I., 25
Burnham, Walter D., 45

Cable Satellite Public Affairs Network
(C-SPAN), 46
Carroll, Mark, 52
Casper, Gerhard, 63
Central Intelligence Agency (CIA), 38,
39
Chang, H.C., 38
Chester, Edward W., 41
Cody, Sue A., 22
Cohen, Morris L., 22
Congressional Information Service
(CIS), 15
Council of Economic Advisors (CEA),
38, 39

Edwards, George C., 8, 23
Elliot, Jeffrey M., 8

Fetzer, Mary, 22
Fisher, Louis, 9

Gallup, George H., 49
Goehlert, Robert U., 10, 23, 61

Graff, Henry F., 9
Gumprecht, Blake, 51

Hyland, Pat, 52

Inter-University Consortium for
Political and Social Research, 43, 55
Israel, Fred L., 35

Jacobstein, J. Myron, 22
Johnson, Donald B., 40

Kane, Joseph N., 6
Kessel, John H., 8
Kurland, Philip B., 63

Levy, Leonard W., 9
Lott, Davis N., 35
Lowery, Roger C., 22

Maisel, Sandy L., 41
Martin, Fenton S., 10, 23, 61
Maxwell, Bruce, 51, 52
McGillivray, Alice V., 42, 44
Mersky, Roy M., 22
Morehead, Joe, 22

National Foreign Assessment Center,
39
National Public Radio, 50
National Security Council, 38, 39
Nelson, Michael, 54

O'Brien, Steven, 7
Office of Management and
  Budget (OMB), 38
Opinion Research Services,
  49

Paletta, Lu Ann, 6
Peterson, Svend, 45
Podell, Janet, 35
Poore, Ben P., 36
Purdue University, 46

Ragsdale, Lyn, 20
Richardson, James D.,
Robinson, Edgar E., 45
Rockman, Bert A., 8
Ryan, Halford, 35

Scammon, Richard M.,
  44
Schnick, Frank L., 52
Schnick, Renee, 52
Shields-West, Eileen,
  42
Singer, Aaron, 35
Smith, Hedrick, 49

Sobel, Robert, 7
Sullivan, Linda, 37

Thomas, G. Scott, 44
Tollefson, Alan M., 38

University of Michigan, 51
U.S. House of Representatives, 40
U.S. Library of Congress, 39, 53
U.S. National Archives and
  Records Service, 63
U.S. Senate, 36
U.S. Supreme Court, 62, 63

Van Geel, Tyll R., 62
Vanderbilt University, 46
Video Insights, 49

Wayne, Stephen J., 23
Whitney, David C., 7
Wilson, Vincent, 6
Wolanin, Thomas R., 38
Wren, Christopher G., 15
Wren, Jill R., 15

Zink, Stephen P., 37

Title Index

ABC POL SCI: A Bibliography of Contents: Political Science and Government, 10

ABC POL SCI on Disc (Compact disk), 13

Almanac of American Politics, 16

Almanac of the Executive Branch, 7

America at the Polls: A Handbook of Presidential Election Statistics 1920–1992, 44

America: History and Life, 11

America: History and Life on Disc (Compact disk), 13

America Votes 21: A Handbook of Contemporary American Election Statistics, 44

American Foreign Policy Index, 29, 34, 38

American Journal of Political Science, 16

American Lobbyists Directory, 47

American Political Leaders: From Colonial Times to the Present, 7

American Political Science Review, 16

American Politics Quarterly, 16

American Presidency: A Bibliography, 10

American Presidency: A Historical Bibliography, 10

American Presidents, 7

American Presidents: A Bibliography, 10

American Public Opinion Index, 49

Annals of Congress, 26

Applied Science and Technology Index, 47

Appointment Book of President Kennedy (1961–1963), 53

Atlantic Monthly, 18

Best Campaign Commercials of 1984 (Video), 50

Best Campaign Commercials of 1988, Presidential General (Video), 50

Best Campaign Commercials of 1988, Presidential Primary (Video), 50

Best Campaign Commercials of 1992, Presidential General (Video), 50

Best Campaign Commercials of 1992, Presidential Primary (Video), 49

Best of Old Campaign Commercials (Video), 50

Bibliography of Presidential Commissions, Committees, Councils, Panels, and Task Forces, 1961–1972, 38

Biographical Directory of the United States Executive Branch, 1774–1989, 7

Book of the Presidents, 6

Broadcast News on CD-ROM (Compact disk), 20, 47

Budget of the United States Government, 38

Budget of the United States Government, Appendix, 39

Business Periodicals Index, 47

Calendars of the United States House of Representatives and History of Legislation, 58

Campaign Speeches of American Presidential Candidates, 1928–1972, 35

Capitol Source, 8

CD/FR: Compact Disk Federal Register (Compact disk), 57

CD Newsbank (Compact disk), 19

CFR Index, 56, 57

CIA Publications Released to the Public through Library of Congress DOCEX: Listing for 1972–1977, 39

CIS Federal Register Index, 29, 30, 32

CIS Five-Year Cumulative Index 1970–1974, 29

CIS Four-Year Cumulative Index 1975–1978, 29

CIS Four-Year Cumulative Index 1979–1982, 29

CIS Four-Year Cumulative Index 1983–1986, 29

CIS Four-Year Cumulative Index 1987–1990, 29

CIS Four-Year Cumulative Index 1991–1994, 29

CIS/Index: Congressional Information Service/Index to Publications of the United States Congress, 29, 32–34, 38

CIS Index to Presidential Executive Orders and Proclamations, 30

CIS Legislative Histories Annual, 29

CIS Presidential Orders and Proclamations, 33

Clearinghouse of Subject-Oriented Internet Resource Guides (WWW site), 51

Code of Federal Regulations, 27, 29, 32, 55–57

Commentary, 18

Common Cause Magazine, 18

Compilation of Messages and Papers of the Presidents, 1789-1927, 26, 32, 33

Congress and the Nation, 5

Congress and the Presidency: A Journal of Capitol Studies, 17

Congress in Print, 59

Congressional Bills, 51

Congressional Globe, 26

Congressional Index, 34, 59

Congressional Masterfile I, 30

Congressional Masterfile II, 30

Congressional Monitor, 59

Congressional Quarterly Almanac, 5, 32, 33

Congressional Quarterly Weekly Report, 17, 31–33, 42, 61

Congressional Record: Proceedings and Debates of the Congress, 26, 32, 33

Congressional Record Scanner, 59

Congressional Roll Call, 59

Congressional Staff Directory, 7

CQ Researcher, 18

CQ's WASHINGTON ALERT (Database), 15, 18, 19, 32, 61

C-SPAN I, 46

C-SPAN II, 46

Cumulated Indexes to the Public Papers of the Presidents, 27

Current, 18

Current Law Index, 11

Daily Diary of President Johnson (1963–1969), 54

DATATIMES (Database), 19

Department of State Bulletin, 26, 30, 34

Diaries of Dwight D. Eisenhower, 1953–1961, 54

Digest of United States Supreme Court Reports, Annotated with Case Annotations, Dissenting and Separate Decisions since 1900, 63

Directory of Washington Lobbyists, Lawyers, and Interest Groups in the Washington Metropolitan Area, 48

Directory of Washington Representatives of American Associations and Industry, 48

Documents of the National Security Council, 1947–1977, 39

Economic Report of the President, 40

Election Data Book: A Statistical Portrait of Voting in America, 43

Encyclopedia of Governmental Advisory Organizations, 37

Encyclopedia of the American Presidency, 9

Executive Agreement Series, 27

Executive Branch (Video), 49

Facts about the Presidents: A Compilation of Biographical and Historical Data, 6

Facts on File, 19

Facts on File News Digest (Compact disk), 20

Federal Advisory Committees, Annual Report of the President, Federal Internet Source, 51

Federal Register, 27, 29, 32, 22, 27, 50, 55, 56

Federal Staff Directory, 7

Federal Staff Directory on Disk (Compact disk), 7

Federal Yellow Book: A Directory of the Federal Departments and Agencies, 8

Franklin D. Roosevelt and Foreign Affairs: Second Series, 1937–1939, 54

Franklin D. Roosevelt: Diary and Itineraries/Usher Books, 54

Fundamentals of Legal Research, 22

Gallup Opinion Index Report: Political, Social and Economic Trends, 49

Gallup Poll: Public Opinion, 1935–1971, 49

Gallup Poll: Public Opinion, 1972–1977, 49

Government Documents Catalog Subscription Service (GDCS) (Compact disk), 15, 30, 38

Government Publications Index on InfoTrac (Compact disk), 15, 38

GPO ACCESS (Database), 32, 51

GPO on Silver Platter (Compact disk), 15, 38

Guide to Political Platforms, 41

Guide to Presidential Advisory Commissions, 1973–1984, 37

Guide to Resources and Services (ICPSR), 55

Guide to the Presidency, 23

Guide to U.S. Elections, 43

Guide to U.S. Government Publications, 37

Harper's Magazine, 18

Harry S Truman Oral Histories Collection, 47

Historic Documents on Presidential Elections 1787–1988, 54

Historic Documents on the Presidency: 1776–1989, 54

How to Access the Federal Government on the Internet: Washington Online, 51

How to Access the Government's Electronic Bulletin Boards: Washington Online, 52

How to Research Congress, 61

Human Events: The National Conservative Weekly, 18

Humanities Index, 11

Humanities Index (Compact disk), 14

Inaugural Addresses of Twentieth-Century American Presidents, 35

Index to Legal Periodicals, 11

Index to Legal Periodicals (Compact disk), 14

InfoTrac (Compact disk), 15

International Economic Report of the President, 40

International Political Science Abstracts, 11

International Political Science Abstracts (Compact disk), 14

Internet Complete Reference, 50

Internet Directory, 50

Internet Sources of Government Information, 51

Introduction to United States Government Information Sources, 22

John F. Kennedy 1960 Campaign, 54

John F. Kennedy Presidential Oral History Collection, 47

Johnson Presidential Press Conferences, 35

Journal of Politics, 16

Judicial Staff Directory, 7

Kennedy Presidential Press Conferences, 36

Landmark Briefs and Arguments of the Supreme Court of the United States: Constitutional Law, 63
Legal Research in a Nutshell, 22
Legal Resources Index, 11
LegalTrac (Compact disk), 14
LEGI-SLATE (Database), 7, 16, 18, 19, 32, 61
LEXIS/NEXIS (Database), 16, 18, 19, 32, 47, 61
List of CFR Sections Affected (LSA), 57

Map Room Messages of President Roosevelt (1942–1945), 53
Map Room Messages of President Truman (1945–1946), 53
MARVEL, 32, 51
Minutes and Documents of the Cabinet Meetings of President Eisenhower (1953–1961), 53
Minutes and Documents of the Cabinet Meetings of President Johnson (1963–1969), 54
Minutes of Meeting of the National Security Council, 39
Monthly Catalog of United States Government Publications, 30, 32–34, 38

National Journal: The Weekly on Politics and Government, 17, 31, 42, 61
National Newspaper Index, 19
National Party Conventions, 1831–1992, 40
National Party Platforms, 40
National Party Platforms of 1980, 40
National Review: A Journal of Fact and Opinion, 18
NES CD-ROM (Compact disk), 43, 55
New Deal Economic Policies: FDR and the Congress, 1933–1938, 54
New Governmental Advisory Organizations, 37
New Republic: A Journal of Opinion, 18
New York Times, 19, 31, 41, 61

NewsBank Index, 19
Newsweek, 41
Nixon Presidential Press Conferences, 36
NYT on Disc (Compact disk), 19

Oral Arguments of the U.S. Supreme Court, 63
Oral Histories of the Johnson Administration, 47

PAIS International (Compact disk), 14
Papers of the Nixon White House, 54
Papers of the President's Science Advisory Committee, 1957–1961, 54
Political Activities of the Johnson White House, 1963–1969, 54
Political Parties and Elections in the United States: An Encyclopedia, 41
Political Research Quarterly, 16
Political Science: Illustrated Search Strategy and Sources with an Introduction to Legal Research for Undergraduates, 22
Politics in America, 16
Polity, 16
Popular Names of U.S. Government Reports: A Catalog, 37
Potsdam Conference Documents, 53
Power Game (Video), 49
Presidency: A Research Guide, 23
Presidency A to Z: A Ready Reference Encyclopedia, 9
President Dwight D. Eisenhower's Office Files, 1953–1961, 54
President Eisenhower's Meetings with Legislative Leaders, 1953–1961, 54
President Franklin D. Roosevelt's Office Files, 1933–1945, 54
President Harry S Truman's Office Files, 1945–1953, 54
President John F. Kennedy's Office Files, 1961–1963, 54
President Kennedy and the Press, 54
Presidential Advisory Commissions: Truman and Nixon, 38
Presidential Ballots, 1836–1892, 45

Presidential Congressional Political Dictionary, 8
Presidential Diaries of Henry Morganthau, Jr. (1938–1945), 53
Presidential Elections: 1789–1992, 43
Presidential Libraries and Museums: An Illustrated Guide, 52
Presidential Primaries and Caucuses: 1992, 42
Presidential Studies Quarterly, 17
Presidential Vetoes, 1789–1988, 36
Presidential Vetoes, 1989–1991, 36
Presidential Vote, 1896–1932, 45
Presidential Vote 1936: Supplementing the Presidential Vote, 1896–1932, 45
Presidents: A Reference History, 9
Presidents Speak: The Inaugural Addresses of American Presidents from Washington to Clinton, 35
Progressive, 18
Public Affairs Chronicle (Compact disk), 46
Public Affairs Information Service Bulletin (PAIS), 12, 33, 41
Public Interest Profiles, 48
Public Papers of the Presidents of the United States, 27, 32, 33
Pursuit of the White House: A Handbook of Presidential Election Statistics and History, 44

Reader's Guide to Periodical Literature, 12, 18, 41
Reader's Guide to Periodical Literature (Compact disk), 14
Records and Briefs, 63
Records of the Presidency: Presidential Papers and Libraries from Washington to Reagan, 52
Register of Debates in Congress, 26
Reports Required by Congress: CIS Guide to Executive Communications, 30
Researching the Presidency: Vital Questions, New Approaches, 8
Role of the Chief Executive (Video), 49
Running for President: The Candidates and Their Images, 41

Social Sciences Citation Index (SSCI), 14
Social Sciences Citation Index Compact Disc Edition (Compact disk), 14
Social Sciences Index, 12
Social Sciences Index (Compact disk), 14
Society: Social Science and Modern Society, 18
SocioFile (Compact disk), 15
Sociological Abstracts, 13
Speeches of the American Presidents, 35
Staff Directories on CD-ROM PLUS (Compact disk), 7
State of the Union Messages of Presidents 1790–1966, 35, 50
Statistical History of the American Presidential Elections, 45
Studying the Presidency, 23
Supreme Court Reporter, 62

Tape Recordings of Oral Arguments before the U.S. Supreme Court, 63
Television News Archives, Vanderbilt University, 46
They Voted for Roosevelt: The Presidential Vote, 1932–1944, 45
THOMAS, 32, 51
TIARA CD-ROM: Treaties and International Agreements Researchers' Archive (Compact Disk), 27, 34
Time: The Weekly Newsmagazine, 19, 41
Title 3, CFR, 27, 32
Treaties and Other International Acts Series, 27, 34
Treaties and Other International Agreements of the United States of America 1776–1949, 25, 34
Treaties in Force, 30, 34
Treaty Series, 27

Understanding Supreme Court Opinions, 62
United States Code, 60
United States Code Annotated, 60

United States Political Science Documents, 13

United States Presidents: Personality and Politics (Video), 49

United States Reports, 62

United States Statutes at Large: Containing the Laws and Concurrent Resolutions Enacted . . . , 31–33

United States Supreme Court Bulletin, 62

United States Supreme Court Digest, 63

United States Supreme Court Reports: Lawyers' Edition, 62

United States Treaties and Other International Agreements, 28, 34

U.S. Budget in Brief, 39

U.S. Code Congressional and Administrative News, 28, 32

U.S. Code on CD-ROM (Compact disk), 60

U.S. Government Manual, 36

U.S. Government Periodicals Index, 13

U.S. Government Periodicals Index (Compact disk), 15

U.S. Law Week, 62

U.S. News and World Report, 19

U.S. President Press Conferences, 35

Using Computers in Legal Research: A Guide to LEXIS and WESTLAW, 15

Veto Messages of the Presidents of the United States, with the Action of Congress Thereon, 36

Vital Speeches of the Day, 34

Vital Statistics on the Presidency: Washington to Clinton, 20, 42

Washington Almanac: A Guide to Federal Policy, 6

Washington Monthly, 19

Washington Post, 19, 31, 41, 61

Washington Post on Disc (Compact disk), 19

Washington Representatives, 48

Weekly Compilation of Presidential Documents, 28, 32, 33, 38

WESTLAW (Database), 16, 18, 19, 32, 61

Westlaw Database List, 16

White House Weekly, 35

Whole Internet: User's Guide and Catalog, 50

Who's Who in the Federal Executive Branch, 8

World Almanac of Presidential Campaigns, 42

World Almanac of Presidential Facts, 6

World Book of America's Presidents, 7

World Wide Web Unleashed, 50